Everyone
Sells!

Congratulations!
— on achieving CLC.

[signature]

Everyone Sells!

HOW TOP PRODUCERS MAKE TOP $$

Lee DuBois

MONOCHROME

SUBSIDIARY OF GRAY MEDIA, INC.
Exeter, New Hampshire

Copyright © 1993 by Monochrome Press, Inc.

All rights reserved. This book or parts thereof may not be reproduced in any form without permission of the publisher.

ISBN: 1-882407-00-8

Library of Congress Catalog Card Number: 93-77146

Designed by Irving Perkins Associates

Manufactured in the United States of America by
Maple-Vail Book Manufacturing Group

10   9   8   7   6   5   4   3   2   1

This book is dedicated to my loving daughter

Dalene DuBois Bradford

*who tirelessly tried to help her father
say what he wanted to say in print*

Contents

CONTENTS

Foreword

WHILE MAKING a sales call on a potential Canadian distributor, our prospect, Samantha Thompson, said, "I really don't think we can market your sales training course because it is too American."

"That is a surprising observation," said my partner, Terry Condrey. "I really never thought of our training in that context. I had always thought of it as Greek."

I stared at him in astonishment!

"Actually," he went on, "some of the principles were first recorded by Plato quoting Socrates on good human communication techniques. Later, a fellow by the name of Franklin . . . Ben Franklin, U.S. ambassador to France, enlarged upon these principles in his autobiography and told of being influenced by Socrates. Then, they were picked up by Lee DuBois and made more contemporary."

Inappropriate as it may have been in this sales setting, I doubled over with laughter. I had never been linked with such illustrious personages.

Condrey's comments about the origin of good sales communication precepts did have a grain of truth. Nothing could be more egotistical than to assume communication ideas or techniques originated with the author or trainer of those principles. Actually, most of them are timeless.

Any teacher will tell you that a principal source of learning comes from those they instruct. I am deeply indebted to the thousands I have trained throughout some 30 years of working with salespeople.

In my formative years in this profession, no one influenced me more than William A. Gayle, Jr., who was the author of *Willie Gayle's Power Selling* and *7 Seconds to Success in Selling*. Without a doubt, Willie was the most superb platform performer and sales instructor that I have ever known. For years, I was a vice president of his corporation, Willie Gayle, Incorporated, until I purchased the rights to the course he developed—"The Willie Gayle Course in Persuasive Speech and Creative Selling."

Also, I had the privilege of training under Mr. Percy Whiting, author of *The Five Great Rules of Selling*, and developer of the original Dale Carnegie Sales Course. Mr. Whiting was truly one of the pioneers in developing a practical course of sales communication techniques.

Therefore, any reference I might make about "my" training should be understood from the proper perspective. Perhaps there might be applications, modifications, interpretations, or examples of selling skills that might be considered "new," but like the laws of physics, *basics* never change! I am but a sum total of these experiences and others, and I humbly and gratefully acknowledge their impact on my work and their contribution to this book.

This book is a direct consequence of the professional sales technique training that I have conducted across the country for over 30 years. It nearly parallels my 16-session videocassette program called "Let the Customer Buy." Should my readers wish a comparison of extra resource material, refer to each chapter's corresponding videotape number in the Guide to *"Let the Customer Buy"* (Appendix A).

What author has not spent hours trying to come up with a name for the book that identifies its content and is eye-catching to a potential reader. Hopefully (using today's vernacular), this title tells it like it is:

EVERYONE SELLS!

How Top Producers Make Top $$

Many reasons for the choice of this title include:

1. Although this book is targeted at those who *sell* for a living, the communication techniques taught herein are applicable to anyone who tries to convince others of the soundness of his or her ideas or proposals.
2. About 80 percent of *all* communication is devoted to selling someone else on accepting the ideas, thoughts, or conclusions of the communicator . . . hence "everyone sells" each and every day!
3. A general lack of knowledge exists about the fact that how-to techniques and principles are available . . . and are identifiable . . . that help the top professional salesperson to make more money. These techniques are transferable and can be learned!
4. Successfully tested professional selling skills enhance the professional image of the salesperson at any point in a career.

This book is a how-to cataloging of professional sales skills and principles developed from over 30 years of sales training experience. It should prove valuable for both salespeople and sales management. Its two major purposes are simple and straightforward:

1. To increase sales substantially.
2. To reduce costly turnover of sales personnel.

Good selling!

Everyone Sells!

CHAPTER 1

Myths and Modern-Day Realities

Plan your work and work your plan!
You have to be motivated to sell.
You have to work hard to be successful in sales.
Have a positive mental attitude.
Never take "NO!" for an answer.
Persistence wins out.
Act enthusiastic and you'll be enthusiastic.
You need to become organized.
If you see enough prospects, you'll make sales.

SOUND FAMILIAR? These myths about selling are prevalent in the sales world—not only prevalent but also a little bit frightening. Look at them closely and consider their implications.

"Plan your work and work your plan." Just work harder, be more organized, and you will sell more?

"Have a positive mental attitude." Smile and the world smiles with you. Be more motivated? Exactly what does being positive really mean?

"Persistence wins out." Making a sale is the only thing that counts—or is it? Where do your client's needs fit in any of these platitudes—or are they really important?

Look at the overall tone of these myths. Do better, work harder, don't give up, act in a certain way. What if you have already tried all these things? What if you have put out all the effort you can muster, and you are still not satisfied with your performance? These golden rules neither offer help nor begin to imply that there are specific skills and strategies you can learn, practice, and apply to improve your selling skills.

Furthermore, what about those seemingly endless company sales meetings? At first, did you look to them to solve some of your problems only to find that they seemed to accentuate the negative? Have these meetings been almost exclusively product-knowledge orientations and pricing updates . . . or were they motivational rah-rah? Have you repeatedly heard exhortations on the need for more business with little help on just how you are expected to accomplish it? Would you rate these sales meetings as the solution to some of your problems or as the cause of them? If these things sound familiar, this book will be like a breath of fresh air.

The purpose of this book is to help you understand what constitutes good selling principles and techniques, not to point out flaws in your approach. This book will provide specific techniques and strategies to improve your effectiveness, regardless of your experience level.

If you are in sales management, this book will show you how to work with your sales force on these same important points. The real benefit to you is that you can increase the sales of your company, and ultimately increase your own income, and do so with less effort!

One of the modern-day realities in the selling profession is that it lacks the definitive, precise language so common in other professions. For example, when professional engineers talk about a project, they speak to one another using unique terminology that enables them to communicate unambiguously. Unless you are an engineer, you might not be able to understand the conversation. This is true in any profession, be it medicine, law, or chemistry.

However, in the sales profession, such precise language is virtually nonexistent. In exasperation, I sometimes label this garbled vocabulary of our profession *vague specifics* or *unknown tongue!*

For example, when a sales manager urges his sales team to "overcome the price objection," just exactly what is he saying? One salesperson might assume argumentative selling was required; another might think the price should be lowered; and yet a third might think the prospect should be outwitted. This is but one small example among hundreds where commonly used words and phrases in our profession lack precise definition. Without accepted definition and a common understanding, analysis of the sales process is impossible. If the sales process cannot be dissected and discussed, it cannot be corrected, taught, and coached.

Once we establish a common vocabulary of important terms used in selling, we will move directly into the science of selling. Breaking it down into manageable pieces, we will dissect the selling process, examining each important step and its function to enhance your communicative skills and improve control, but not obvious control, in each interview.

Contrary to your expectations, perhaps, we will *begin* with the closing step! We'll get to the bottom line early, you might say, and to the part of selling that seemingly causes the most anxiety. We'll prove it to be the easiest step of the sale to accomplish.

However, our work will not end here, for just being able to identify the discrete actions and set of choices facing a salesperson is not enough. We will analyze the techniques that are available to you to help solve the myriad selling problems encountered each and every selling day. We will examine their appropriateness in fact-finding, first approach, arousing curiosity, conviction, handling objections, creating desire and numerous other selling techniques that will supply you with an arsenal of professional communications skills. You will be able to use these skills sequentially or separately. The real benefit to you will be becoming armed

5

to face the toughest sale and to handle it easier than you can now imagine.

Let's now begin by developing a common sales vocabulary that will enable us to communicate clearly, and will allow you to communicate with other sales professionals. We will identify the most innocent of sales terms used by all of us and be absolutely certain of each word meaning.

- What does it mean *to sell* anyway?
- What is the difference between *professionalism* and *high-pressure* tactics?
- Just how important is a *positive mental attitude?* What is *enthusiasm* and how do you get it?
- Should a professional salesperson be *empathetic?*

WHAT IS SELLING?

On my first training assignment in Australia, I was concerned about cultural differences which might hinder my effectiveness with the local sales force. I decided to start with definitions early in the seminar so that I might communicate more readily. I began by asking the audience to define *selling*. The silence was deafening.

"What is it that we salespeople try to do each day?" I asked. Again, there was no response. I was so surprised that I tried this same question back in the States and encountered the very same reaction.

Can you define the word? After a little prodding in my seminars, answers are cautiously ventured, like *persuade, convince,* or *give benefits.* Interestingly, few people recognize that *80 percent of ALL communication is selling.* If one truly understands the meaning of the word, it becomes apparent that all human beings are *selling* something in most of their conversations. Everybody sells, only you and I happen to do it for a living!

Let's consider some definitions of *selling* that are practical for our use:

- Selling is the ability to get a decision in your favor.
- Selling is the ability to get someone else to do something you want them to do because you've convinced them *they want to do it.*
- Selling is the ability to communicate your product's technical features and benefits in layman's terms so your prospect can make an intelligent decision as to whether or not to buy.

PROFESSIONALISM VERSUS HIGH PRESSURE

Certainly, you believe you are in an honorable profession. The wheels of the economy are geared to the direct results of salesmanship. Too often our professional image is denigrated by the misunderstanding of exactly what constitutes *high pressure*. A distinctive definition of this phrase needs our concentration and understanding.

Few things annoy me more than to hear one say, "I'm *just* a salesperson." In my classes, I usually ask for a show of hands of those who consider themselves professional. All hands will show. I then ask how many want to be considered high pressure, and no one responds. However, when I ask them for the difference, they all appear puzzled and inarticulate!

Professional

- Professionals have specific skills and expertise to call upon to serve their clients.

7

- Professional salespeople think in terms of their *prospect's* interest—first, last, and always.

High Pressure

- High-pressure salespeople are amateurs.
- High-pressure salespeople think in terms of their *own* interest—first, last, and always.

High-pressure tactics give the selling profession a very bad image. High-pressure salespeople tend to speak down to prospect's in an insulting manner. Usually, these salespeople are overly persistent and sometimes very rude.

What separates the professional salesperson from the high-pressure salesperson is motive as *discerned by the prospect!* This means that you, too, can be considered high pressure if the prospect feels you are putting your own interest first. The professional techniques outlined in this book will help you to develop and maintain your professional image.

It is sad to note that if high-pressure salespeople knew of professional sales techniques, they would be much more successful and be able to serve their clients at the same time.

POSITIVE MENTAL ATTITUDE

Hundreds of sales rallies expound the virtues of having a positive mental attitude. Yet, on critical examination, I have found very few who can define exactly what *positive* really means. *Positive* falls into the category of a *vague specific*—a seemingly important, but useless phrase.

Can you tell me what it means, and, more importantly, just how to get it? Far too many people earnestly seeking help in selling have been turned off by the great motivators who expound the virtues of a positive attitude in selling.

Do yourself a favor. From now on, whenever you hear the phrase *Positive Mental Attitude* mentally change it to *CONFIDENT Mental Attitude!* If you sense an attitude problem and identify it as lack of confidence, perhaps you will seek to identify the source. Then, and only then, can you start to correct the problem and improve your attitude.

Do you begin with the right attitude and become confident, or does confidence beget the right attitude? It is somewhat like the proverbial question of which comes first—the chicken or the egg? Only, in this case, the question is easy to answer: *Confidence* comes before the right *attitude!* A salesperson with the right mental attitude in selling exudes confidence in what he or she does. To improve your attitude, first determine what skill is required to improve your confidence level. Perfect that skill and a confident mental attitude is sure to follow.

ENTHUSIASM

"Act enthusiastic and you'll be enthusiastic," championed Dale Carnegie. Thousands, if not millions, have quoted him. The problem inherent in this generalism is that it seems to suggest you can falsely portray emotions you do not feel and thereby sell more effectively. Real enthusiasm cannot be faked.

What is enthusiasm, exactly, and how can it be attained? This very important quality of a professional salesperson needs to be defined, analyzed, and learned! Enthusiasm is an essential characteristic of a successful salesperson, and should be present in every interview. Consider the meaning of the word:

Enthusiasm comes from the Greek word *entheos* ("God within"). It is an emotion from within that can be electrifying and inspiring.

9

If you should find a need to be more enthusiastic in your selling interview, it is important for you to know what causes it. Sales enthusiasm is derived from two sources. You will be enthusiastic if you have:

1. A sufficient knowledge of your product or service.
2. A deep belief in the *miracles* [my word] your product or service can provide your prospect.

If you sense your enthusiasm is waning, simply ask yourself two simple questions:

1. Do I understand my product well enough to explain it to the prospect?
2. Do I *really believe* it is right for the prospect?

If you can answer both questions affirmatively, you will be enthusiastic!

Being enthusiastic in the sales interview does *not* mean unending cheerfulness. It does not suggest an artificially pumped-up demeanor such as displayed on television car advertisements. It does imply a heartfelt conviction about one's product or service.

Enthusiasm has varying degrees. If you exhibit too much enthusiasm, it is possible to turn off the prospect quickly. The rule of thumb is that you should be "one degree" more enthusiastic than your prospect. During the selling process, you work to elevate the prospect's enthusiasm degree by degree by using good selling procedures. You do this until the prospect becomes nearly as enthusiastic as you.

Becoming enthusiastic is relatively simple as long as you know and believe in what you sell. As a trainer, I am much more concerned about your ability to make your prospect enthusiastic than I am about your ability to maintain enthusiasm. This ability takes professional selling skills that we will explore in detail as we proceed through this book.

EMPATHY

The most important obligation of any professional salesperson is to develop the objectivity and concern necessary to be empathetic with the prospect. Empathy is the badge of the professional. It is the personification of objectivity. It requires the exercise of extremely sensitive, conscientious listening.

Empathy is another word in our selling profession that I find few salespeople able to define:

> *Empathy* means the ability to put yourself in the other person's shoes *without becoming emotionally involved.*

Empathy is not to be confused with sympathy. If you sympathize with your prospects, they have sold you . . . you haven't sold them! Sympathy is putting yourself in other people's shoes and *agreeing* with them or feeling sorry for them. Empathy means sensing their feelings, understanding them, but remaining unemotionally objective about your recommendation.

Whether you realize it or not, you expect empathy, or objectivity, from other professionals, such as your doctor or lawyer. Your prospect should expect the same from you!

Following this line of reasoning, let's consider the surgeon. Do you suppose a doctor can understand how you feel if you do not want to take the advice of going to the hospital for surgery? Yet, the doctor would remain unemotional (and probably quite persistent!) in insisting on the necessity. Empathy is the most important service a professional can provide a client!

Now, let us better understand the role of empathy with a practical example. Have you ever seen something you really wanted to buy but felt you simply couldn't *afford*? Then, if a prospect should say to you, "I can't afford it," can you understand how he or she feels? If you really believe your proposal is right for the prospect, you would sense this feeling but *empathetically* continue to sell. Objectively, you would try to get across the point, in the prospect's best interest, that he or she can't afford to be *without it*. This is your professional responsibility in selling.

CHAPTER SUMMARY

In summary, our selling profession seems to abound in myths, misconceptions, and preconceived notions of what constitutes good selling practices. It is inconceivable that our sales profession has not been given the attention it deserves to develop and mature into a modern communication science to aid the salesperson. The realities in our modern business world are:

- Sales training is usually done haphazardly, if at all.
- Many misconceptions abound as to what constitutes good selling skills and practices.
- Too many salespeople are left on their own to develop sales techniques.
- Lack of identification of successful sales procedures is the cause of their rarely being transferable.
- Too many companies try to hire experienced sales representatives rather than to prioritize training as a continuous process for their salespeople.
- Salespeople are rarely trained to analyze their own successes and failures so that greater sales can result.

A major effort will be made in this book to remove the myths and misconceptions from the selling profession, and replace them with time-tested ideas, skills, and techniques. We will take the mystery out of our profession and prove selling can be fun, simple, precise, and much more profitable!

Reflecting on this chapter, review in your mind some of the concepts and premises that form a cornerstone to a more precise understanding of the selling profession. For example:

- Many commonly used terms in the selling profession need more precise definitions so that salespeople can analyze their presentations and make needed improvements.
- See if you can now define:
  —Selling
  —Professionalism
  —High pressure
  —Enthusiasm
  —Positive mental attitude
  —Empathy

Before we start our professional selling adventure, I'm going to ask you to take a moment to answer an important question. I have asked this of literally thousands of salespeople and of sales management before training them:

What do you *believe* is a salesperson's biggest problem in the field?

Does my question cause you to be wary? Do you have a biased viewpoint? Surely you have an opinion, and that opinion is important to your progress in this book.

The question is not intended to be provocative but to serve as a starting point in the development of additional skills peculiar to your own needs. It is hoped you stated what you believe is your *own* problem (or if you are in management, your experiences with your sales team dictate your answer!). Later on, you will discover the importance of identifying your own unique perspective in considering this question.

With this question, I am asking you to start to identify your own understanding, beliefs, and experiences regarding what constitutes good selling procedures. Any problems of which we are aware serve as a starting point for progress. One can more easily measure progress first by identifying obstacles to greater success and then by methodically solving them.

CHAPTER 2

It's the Law!

As IMPORTANT as the laws of physics can be for the professional engineer, two laws of communication are vital to the salesperson. These laws can mean the difference between success and failure in the selling interview. The use of these laws can separate a sophisticated salesperson from a mediocre one. This chapter will be devoted to understanding the implications of these two laws—the Law of Psychological Reciprocity and the Law of Challenging Belief.

Years ago, a salesman in one of my classes gave me a book on selling. The book's title, *The New Psychology of Persuasion and Motivation in Selling*, was so intimidating I had to force myself to start reading it. Once past the title, I discovered a book that has been an immense help to me in training salespeople.

The three authors, Robert Whitney, Thomas Hubin, and John Murphy, first caught my interest when they proposed that salespeople would be much more successful in communication if they complied with a law entitled the Law of Psychological Reciprocity. They asserted this law is like a physics law. It is an absolute; it *always works!* Here is the law:

LAW OF PSYCHOLOGICAL RECIPROCITY

Anytime you give another person credit for his or her intelligence, that person is automatically, morally, and subconsciously bound to give you credit for the next thing you say!

Certainly, a professional sells more effectively by asking questions than by making factual statements. Therefore, asking questions and listening to the answers becomes one way to give the prospect credit for intelligence. Coincidentally, your prospect becomes automatically, morally, and subconsciously bound to give you credit for the next *thing* you say. Your credibility builds, and your chance to make a sale increases.

This law works on prospects, friends, husbands, wives, children . . . everybody! As you study this law, you begin to comprehend the implications of its ability to help you build better relationships in all communication.

Any good salesperson must be a good listener. The more questions you ask the prospect . . . and the better you listen . . . the more prospects have the feeling you are giving them credit for intelligence. When you do your preliminary fact-finding, and listen carefully to your prospect's answers, you are giving the prospect credit for intelligence. When a prospect voices an objection, and you listen alertly for the motivation behind the objection, you give a prospect credit for intelligence.

In fact, the more I used this important law, the more I understood why the selling techniques that I had been teaching for years worked so well. I discovered that most of the selling skills we cover in this book, by their very nature, give prospects credit for their intelligence. I had been teaching selling principles and skills for many years without really understanding exactly why they worked!

Also in the book *The New Psychology of Persuasion and Motivation in Selling*, an entire chapter is devoted to this question: "What do you believe is a salesperson's biggest problem in the field?" The #1 problem of salespeople was unlike any I have ever seen. Most salespeople falter because they *challenge the beliefs of their prospects*.

Throughout this book, we develop specific questions to enable you to avoid challenging your prospect's beliefs. These questions will help you to remain in command, but not obvious command, of your interviews.

This instinct for avoiding argumentativeness in selling is confirmed and dramatically emphasized in the second important law of communication:

LAW OF CHALLENGING BELIEF

Never directly challenge another person's belief, but make what you say consistent with what he or she already believes!

Do you challenge the beliefs of your prospects? Is this your biggest problem in sales? "Surely not!" I thought when answering for myself. However, as I read on, I began to wonder.

I decided to find out! My prospects were my students whom I was selling (teaching) each week in 11 weekly sessions. Was it possible that I was challenging the beliefs of my students? With my many years of experience, didn't I know better than they what was important for them to learn so that they could be more successful in the field?

I surveyed each and every class, composed of both sales management and salespeople, at the start of the first session. I've followed this procedure in dozens, if not hundreds, of classes. I ask:

What do you *believe* is a salesperson's biggest problem in the field?

To better understand my audience, I also ask for their total number of years of sales experience and whether or not they are in management.

To my amazement, I found their answers did not always match my assessment of their needs. When I targeted my instruction more directly to their needs, I sensed their learning improved dramatically. The selling principles I taught were accepted more readily when I kept their answers to this question in mind during the sessions and didn't challenge that belief. At the same time, I was complying with the Law of Psychological Reciprocity and giving them credit for their intelligence! Teaching became easier for me, and my classes considered the training more relevant.

Before I began to use the surveys, I had *assumed* that I was experienced enough to know my students' needs and put myself in the position of challenging their beliefs. Fine-tuning my presentations to respond to the beliefs of each class, and even to individual views within the class, made a significant contribution to the success of selling them on using the information presented.

Speaking of challenging beliefs, it seems appropriate to share a revelation of difference in beliefs revealed by my surveys of classes. After several years of accumulating responses, I decided to tabulate them. I separated the responses of sales management from salespeople. Comparison of the statistics uncovered a heretofore unrecognized communication gap. Not only were the responses of the two groups totally different, they were very nearly reversed in priority! At first, I didn't believe, nor comprehend, what I was seeing.

Let's look at the Sales Management Survey first.

SALES MANAGEMENT SURVEY

(Average years of selling experience: 17.7, from 2 to 40 years)

Question: *What Do You Believe Is a Salesperson's Biggest Problem in the Field?*

Poor work habits, lack of activity, self-discipline, organization	30.0%
Lack of motivation or desire	26.9%
Prospecting	14.4%
Call reluctance	8.3%
Poor attitude	6.6%
Problems in presentation	5.4%
Closing the sale	4.8%
First approach	1.8%
Lack of self-confidence	1.2%
Product knowledge	0.6%

Study the results carefully, and decide whether or not your sales management team would have answered the survey similarly. Surely these problems as seen by management become a major emphasis in what is covered in sales meetings. Reexamine your own answer to the question in Chapter 1 and see if you agree with management.

I remember tabulating the Sales Management Survey first. I also remember agreeing with their perspective! Was I ever in for a surprise when I tabulated the survey from the salespeople.

SALESPERSON SURVEY

(Average years of selling experience: 9.45, from 0 to 40 years)

Question: *What Do You Believe Is a Salesperson's Biggest Problem in the Field?*

Closing the sale	35.82%
Prospecting	32.53%
First approach	10.05%
Handling objections	9.60%
Getting the interview	4.80%
Call reluctance	2.40%
Attitude	2.40%
Organization	0.96%
Presentation	0.96%
Product knowledge	0.48%

Notice the difference in the two surveys! How can they be so different, and why? No wonder the boss sometimes misunderstands you! Look again at the two surveys and compare priorities. Have you ever disagreed with statements made by management as to just what is wrong with sales production? A careful comparison of the two surveys identifies a serious communication problem!

Several important lessons can be learned. One lesson might be to develop a better perspective in understanding your colleagues. Sales management and salespeople *look at the same problem differently*. It is not a matter of who is right or who is wrong. It is a matter of a difference in perspective. It is a matter of two sets of beliefs—beliefs about training needs—that meet on the sales field in a collision course!

The two surveys provide very practical insights into why sales management may provide sales training that does not agree with salespeople's needs. Notice that the first three items in the Sales Management Survey represent the view of 71 percent of all questioned. The kind of training, seen from this perspective, would emphasize time management, motivation, and calling upon more prospects. Training based on the Salesperson Survey, on the other hand, would be based on the techniques of selling!

The first five items in the Salesperson Survey total almost 93 percent of the respondents. These jump out from the page once you recognize all five items can be preceded with just two words—*how-to!*

The salespeople are, in effect, saying, "I want to know *how-to* close, *how-to* prospect, *how-to* make a first approach, *how-to* handle objections, and *how-to* get the interview." You cannot use these two words to precede the first three items on the Sales Management Survey.

This difference of perspective is dramatic! It becomes apparent that salespeople see the *problem*, while management sees the *effect* of the problem. Management senses the symptoms, while salespeople understand the disease. Moral? Once management solves the salespeople's problems, they will also solve their own!

You now have the basis to understand why management provides so many motivational meetings with the hope to inspire their salespeople. It is because they *believe* lack of motivation is a major problem. Add up all the items on the Sales Management

Survey that are *attitudinal* in nature—they total 43 percent. Salespeople, whose beliefs are different, soon tire of these meetings and say they don't work.

What salespeople say does work is training on proven sales techniques, such as those described in this book. The path to self-motivation comes from solving those problems shown in the Salesperson Survey through proficiency in habitually using good selling skills!

Based on the surprising answers received from one innocent question to sales management and salespeople, are you now so absolutely *sure* that you know the beliefs of *your* prospects? Is it possible that you, too, have been challenging their beliefs? What have you done during your interviews to be certain that your presentation is relevant to your prospect's needs? How conscientiously have you been listening, and just exactly how much empathy have you employed?

What other ways can the two important laws have practical application for you? The Law of Challenging Belief, for example, infers you should resist arguing with the prospects. With a friend, you might debate a disagreement, but with a prospect, the common wisdom is to avoid confrontation. "Win an argument, lose a sale," we are told.

An experienced salesperson would never answer an objection with an overt challenge, such as: "You're wrong, stupid!" even though one might feel that way at times.

However, we inadvertently challenge the beliefs of prospects in many other, subtler ways. Consider phrases such as: "Yes, but," or "Yes, however." These innocuous, and common, comebacks are not only argumentative, they're dangerous. In effect, you signal to the prospect, "Yes, but you are wrong!" These hidden challenges are deadly and can derail a sales interview. A challenged prospect is less likely to listen or communicate freely.

In later chapters on handling, classifying, and analyzing objections, you will improve your techniques in complying with both laws of communication. The real benefit to you is that selling becomes easier and more fun.

Be aware that ignorance of the Law of Challenging Belief can cause you to lose sales! The outward simplicity of this law belies its importance and its ease of use. I wish that I could tell you it is as easy to comply with this law as it is to say it, but it isn't. The more you try to comply with this law, the more apparent it becomes how well you need to know your prospects to really understand their beliefs. I asked you earlier: "Do you really know what your prospects believe?" What is their attitude toward you, your company, your product, and the key points of your presentation? Is your presentation intimately geared to their wants, needs, and desires? Is it consistent with their goals and objectives?

Careful interpretation of the two laws can also suggest why "canned" presentations do not always work. Verbatim sales talks cannot possibly be unilaterally right for all prospects. Prospects' beliefs can be so different that one memorized presentation cannot possibly work all the time. Besides, such mechanical sales talks rarely give prospects credit for intelligence. However, "prepared" presentations, such as the examples throughout this book, are successful. This kind of presentation includes probing questions that allow distinct beliefs to be uncovered and give prospects credit for their intelligence at the same time.

So, where do we go from here? The answer is self-evident if you study the remaining chapter titles! We will concentrate on the *how-to* of selling to solve the salespeople's problems. We'll accomplish two objectives simultaneously, since the end result of helping salespeople with proven sales skills ultimately solves many of management's problems, too.

It is hoped we have laid the groundwork in communication so we can concentrate on selling skills and principles. In fact, in the next chapter, I am going to do something very unusual by concentrating on the end of the selling presentation *first*—"Closing the Sale!"

Why, in a sales technique book, should we start with closing? ... because nearly 36 percent of the salespeople in the survey reported closing the sale as the biggest problem! Therefore, giving them credit for their intelligence, and yours, too, we'll solve this problem early and prove how easy the closing step really is! The real benefit to you will be more sales and more commissions right away. Then, perhaps, you will be morally, and subconsciously bound to accept the fact that other sales techniques are as important, if not more important, to your success.

CHAPTER SUMMARY

After many years of training salespeople, I discovered a question that makes each of my meetings a success. It is my sincere hope that this same question might help to make each chapter of this book a success for you. *Please take a moment at the end of each chapter to answer it for yourself!*

What was the one most important idea you received from this chapter, and how are you going to apply it today?

Some of the more important points were:

- Use of the Law of Psychological Reciprocity helps you to understand better your prospects' needs while, at the same time, committing them to accept more readily what you say.
- Use of the Law of Challenging Belief is a sure way to sense and to avoid conflict with your prospect. It helps you mentally to get on the side of your prospect and sense any conflicts that might arise in the interview, thereby diminishing their negative impact.

CHAPTER 3

The "Secret" of Closing the Sale

IT SEEMS strange to be talking about the "secret" of closing after having taught it for so many years. Surely, the secret is out. However, each time I appear before salespeople and sales management to teach the basics of closing a sale, the simple ideas seem to electrify the audience. The old misconceptions of what it means "to close" still prevail.

What are your beliefs and understandings about closing? Consider your own answers to the following questions:

- When should you close a sale?
- How often should you close in an interview?
- What happens if you ask for the order too early?
- Have you ever heard of a Trial Close and can you define the term?
- What is the difference between a Trial Close and an Order-Asking Question?
- Why are salespeople often apprehensive about closing?

The correct answers to these questions about closing will help to eliminate any indecision or apprehension in the closing process. The purpose of this chapter is to make closing easier, more profitable, and more fun. To the professional salesperson, closing is the simplest part of the selling interview. It is as easy as falling off a log!

First, let's tackle the question of the correct *time* to close a sale. Technically, there is but one time, and it is when the prospect has already bought. My words are chosen very carefully. I did not say, "When the prospect is ready to buy." I said, "When the prospect has *already bought!*"

That brings up a question. The question is: "How do you know when the prospect has bought?" If you don't know, one of the most effective means of determining this is with the use of Trial Closes.

Graduates of my training report they have increased their sales by at least 15 percent by learning to use Trial Closes, and that they have reduced their selling time by as much as 50 percent! A technique this successful needs to be identified precisely and understood. If you feel you are already familiar with the term, before reading further, please write two Trial Closes on a separate sheet of paper.

The term *Trial Close* is really a misnomer because it implies *trying to close*. Normally, when I ask for Trial Closes, I get the following:

Would you like the red or the green?
Shall we order a gross?
Can you see the doctor Monday for the physical?
Would you like to make an offer for this home?
Would you like to purchase this at market price?

Actually, the above questions are excellent Order-Asking Questions rather than Trial Closes. They should be used *only* when the prospect has already bought. It is a very common mistake for salespeople to confuse the two terms, and this confusion can cost them sales.

First, then, let's define Order-Asking Questions and state their purpose. The *Order-Asking Question* asks for a *decision*, and should be used only when the prospect has already bought. Its purpose

25

is to let the prospect know what you as the salesperson already know—that the decision has been made. Technically speaking, it is NOT to be used to *get the order*, because your selling that preceded the Order-Asking Question has done that! If you read the responses again, you will recognize each asks for a decision.

Think now! What would happen if you ask for a decision *too early* in the interview? It should be apparent that if your question is premature, you may lose the sale. The exact timing of an Order-Asking Question is very important. Salespeople instinctively sense this, and, therefore, it is a possible cause for their anxiety at the moment of closing.

The rule is this: Never ask for the order, or decision, unless the prospect is *ready to buy* . . . or to be even more precise, unless the prospect has *already bought!*

This leads us to the important *difference* between an Order-Asking Question and a Trial Close. This difference, once properly understood, produces excitement in even the more experienced salespeople when they discover when and how to use each instrument. It causes everyone to lose the fear of closing the sale:

An Order-Asking Question asks for a *decision*.
A Trial Close asks for an *opinion!*

What do you suppose is the *purpose* of a Trial Close? It is to determine whether your prospect understands and accepts your proposal. It is a means of determining when you should use an Order-Asking Question.

Putting it another way, a Trial Close takes the *temperature* of the prospect toward buying your product or service. You will find whether he or she is cold, warm, or hot toward buying. If *hot*, you *accept* the order. A Trial Close can be called a salesperson's thermometer.

Please note: Again, I'm choosing my words carefully. If the prospect is *hot* toward buying, you know the decision has been made. You simply *accept* what you already know. You accept the prospect's decision to buy. There is no high-pressure, arm-twisting gimmick involved. A professional salesperson lets the prospect buy.

Since Trial Closes should ask for an opinion, we will take advantage of this definition, and revelation, by giving you a very successful technique. You need only to precede your probing questions with six important words: *"In your opinion, do you feel . . ."* When you use these words, you will know you are *always* using Trial Closes.

Let's return to the five Order-Asking Questions and convert each to a Trial Close using, *"In your opinion, do you feel . . .":*

"In your opinion, do you feel you prefer the red or the green color?"

"In your opinion, do you feel the gross price is advantageous to you?"

"In your opinion, do you feel Monday is a good day for your appointment for a physical?"

"In your opinion, do you feel you would like to make an offer on this home?"

"In your opinion, do you feel you would like to place your order at the market price?"

Question: When should you ask for a decision? Answer: Only when the prospect has already bought.

Question: When should you ask for an opinion? Answer: ANYTIME!

I have found that almost all of the salespeople I have trained already know how to ask for the order. Most problems seem to occur because of the *timing* of the Order-Asking Question.

Therefore, the secret to closing, or asking for a decision, is not *how* but *when* . . . and the proper use of a

27

Trial Close is an excellent tool to determine *when* to ask for the order.

Whenever you ask for a prospect's opinion, you give credit for intelligence, and you lower the risk of challenging beliefs. You will find that prospects love to give you their opinion. You may not always like their opinion, but they will gladly give it to you!

Conscientiously listening to the replies from your Trial Closes often makes you aware of the buying decision before the prospect knows about it. Therefore, it is the Order-Asking Question that subtly alerts your prospect to his or her commitment.

There is nothing mystical about closing. A good closer is simply, and above all, a skilled salesperson! I repeat, the Order-Asking Question doesn't magically cause the prospect to buy. It is the selling you have done previously that persuades the prospect to buy. Constantly probing with Trial Closes alerts you to the fact that the sale has been made.

The six words—*"In your opinion, do you feel—"* that act as a thermometer allow you literally to take the buying temperature of the prospect. You will receive one of three responses with a Trial Close, and they are:

yes
maybe
no!

If you hear a "yes" to your question, you can pretty well assume the prospect agrees with you and has "bought." If you receive a "maybe," there is an indication of need for further information. If the answer is "no!" you may find that much more selling is required. Or, you may discover you are completely on the wrong track, presenting the incorrect benefits for this particular prospect. More conscientious listening in this situation is a must.

After all, when would you rather get a "no!" . . . early or late in the interview? Of course, the answer is "early!" Using Trial Closes throughout the interview, you will get any negatives out early so that you can more effectively handle them. Incidentally, even though you get a "no!" the Trial Close is still working for you, providing invaluable feedback as to where you are in the selling process.

Another great advantage of using Trial Closes is to remove pressure from the prospect by converting premature Order-Asking Questions into Opinion-Asking Questions. Remember, it is easy for prospects to give you their opinions. On the other hand, it is difficult to make a decision.

"So what?" you might protest. "This is just semantics when you proceed with, '*In your opinion, do you feel . . .*' " How right you are. Effective selling communication demands the proper use of semantics. You will be amazed how this selling thermometer will help you.

Let's hypothetically examine the mental reaction a professional salesperson might have when three different responses to the same question are received.

In your opinion, do you feel you prefer the red or the green color?

PROSPECT: Really, I like the yellow better!
 (Oh! Oh! The sale is already made!)
PROSPECT: Well, I think I'll look around before I choose.
 (Perhaps I had better be more certain of the prospect's preferences.)
PROSPECT: Don't rush me! I don't intend to make a decision today.
SALESPERSON: I'm sorry, I wasn't asking for a decision. But were you to make a choice today, tomorrow, or a week from now would your preference be red or green?

In the last situation, the salesperson's response is very appropriate and not at all manipulative. With the use of the word *opinion*, no decision was solicited. Within a second, the salesperson recognizes the temperature of the prospect toward buying . . . it is cold!

Getting a "no!" certainly doesn't mean the salesperson should give up. On the contrary, if a salesperson feels empathetically that the prospect needs more objective information upon which to make a wise decision, there is a professional obligation to keep on selling. In many instances, no rejection is implied by the prospect. Only an opinion is rendered. More importantly, the prospect gives this opinion without feeling the slightest pressure for any final decision.

In your opinion, do you feel you would be more in command, but not obvious command, by frequently using Trial Closes throughout your presentations? I trust your answer is an enthusiastic "yes!"

It is important to caution you not to change the wording. Do not use, "In your opinion, do you *think* . . . " Prospects hate to think! The word *think* causes them to seek a profound, thoughtful answer. You are not looking for a profound answer; you simply want to know how they feel.

Nor do you want to use the phrase, "In your opinion, *don't* you feel . . . " The word *don't* tends to send the message they should agree with you. You are not asking them to agree with you; you sincerely want to know *how they feel*.

Several years ago in Baltimore, Maryland, a real estate broker named Frank Miano was a student in my class. The week after we had discussed Trial Closes, he returned excited, wanting to tell us about his experience with, *"In your opinion, do you feel . . ."* Frank shared his experience of working an open house the previous Sunday.

"As I started to lock up for the evening, a young family drove up. The kids were bawling and the father cursing.

The wife insisted, "Oh, while we are here, let's just look at this one more house."

Tired after the long day, and not really expecting this weary bunch to be good prospects, I decided to make the best of the situation by practicing my newly learned sales technique and decided to use only Trial Closes in the interview.

"*In your opinion, do you feel* your sofa would fit in this living room?" I asked the husband.

"I am so tired of looking at houses that I don't care whether it would or not!" was his response.

I thought, "Well, that's one," and started counting the Trial Closes on my fingers behind my back.

"*In your opinion, do you feel* there would be sufficient cabinet space for your dishes," I asked the wife, as they toured the kitchen.

"There was a lot more room for them in the house we just saw down the street," she said.

"That's two!" I thought.

I went through every room of the house asking and counting Trial Closes. To my amazement, the couple committed to a contract for the house on the 14th Trial Close without any other selling on my part!"

"I couldn't believe it!" he told the class.

Can you imagine what this family must have heard from other real estate agents all day long? "Don't you just *love* this house!" . . . "This house has such a marvelous view!" . . . "Don't you think the yard is spacious!" . . . "This is the best bargain in this area!" . . . No doubt they heard superlative after superlative. No wonder they were worn out and cranky. No one, until Frank, had sought their opinions or given them credit for their intelligence.

Salespeople often talk themselves out of more sales than they talk themselves into. Too many salespeople sell a product in one minute and buy it back in the next ten by talking too much. With the use of Trial Closes, you lessen the chances of this happening!

Remember, with Trial Closes you are *not* trying to close. You

31

simply are trying to ascertain the prospect's acceptance of what you are proposing.

This leads me to a very important caution. An enthusiastic "yes!" by the prospect may mean the sale is made, but it could also mean that only one feature or benefit is decided upon. It may be important to further test with additional Trial Closes before you accept the order.

During every class on Trial Closes, I am asked how many can be used in an interview. The correct answer is that there is no limit to the number. People accept repeated requests for their opinions and, in many cases, become friendlier.

Why do some salespeople fear the closing process? It seems to be related directly to the fear of rejection. Sometimes, this fear stems from previous unsuccessful experiences caused by asking for the order at the wrong time. With your repeated use of Trial Closes, you never risk this happening!

For the next week, I challenge you to use at least *seven* Trial Closes in each of your interviews. I have been told this technique alone increases sales by 15 percent. Isn't it worth a try?

CLOSING THE SALE

You should now be able to distinguish the precise difference between closing and trial closing. With the title "The 'Secret' of Closing the Sale," we are moving into Order-Asking Questions. In other words, we start dealing with the *finesse* of getting a prospect's decision. A professional salesperson learns not to be heavy-handed in this procedure in order to relieve any trauma a prospect may experience in making a decision.

Order-Asking Questions should ask for *minor decisions*, meaning they should be "light" in weight. This helps to keep the decision-making process from being an unnecessary burden for the prospect.

What is the exact *purpose* of an Order-Asking Question for a truly professional salesperson? It may surprise you to know it is NOT to get the order.

We learned earlier to ask for the order after the prospect has bought, as determined from our Trial Closes. Therefore, *you already know* he or she has bought! The real purpose is to let the prospect know what you have already discovered.

When the prospect suddenly recognizes having made a decision after affirmatively answering your Order-Asking Question, your demeanor is important. In an easy, relaxed manner, you simply "iron out" the remaining details. This assumptive manner helps to relax and reassure the prospect the decision was wise.

Any professional knows that making a decision can be traumatic. Think about the biggest buying decision you have ever made. Perhaps, it was the purchase of a house or car. Can you remember your anxiety right up to the moment you made the commitment?

This trauma, if left unchecked, can lead to what is called *buyer's remorse* and even cause the canceling of a contract. In most cases, buyer's remorse can be avoided if the salesperson diminishes the impact of the decision with the use of proper Order-Asking Questions.

Salespeople have been startled, in some cases, to see the prospect temperamentally explode or jump up from behind a desk and pace or show other signs of anxiety at the moment of decision. This demeanor, called a *moment of insanity* by psychologists, can be caused by the anxiety of making the decision.

If this sounds like an exaggeration, consider the pressures of an everyday occurrence that you have experienced. Having a quick lunch with friends, you notice everyone staring at the menu, unable to make a decision. Finally, someone will say, "I guess I'll have a hamburger," and everybody else orders a hamburger just to avoid making a decision!

Now, if it is that difficult to decide what to eat, how much more difficult do you feel it might be for our prospects to commit to purchasing our products? Decisions on some products may mean the investment of a major portion of the life savings of the prospect. Is it any wonder it can be traumatic at times? It is our professional responsibility to diminish this impact with easy-to-answer Order-Asking Questions.

Let's look at some examples of *minor* Order-Asking Questions, made easy for a prospect to answer:

> "Do you want your middle initial listed on the title, or should I leave it out?"
> "Would a Monday delivery be soon enough?"
> "Do you want to use your MasterCard?"

An affirmative answer to these questions, minor in context, lets prospects know of their decision on the complete proposal.

Now, for diversity and for more finesse in closing, let's consider several different categories of Order-Asking Questions.

Alternate proposal
Minor point
Impending doom
Extra inducement
The instruction
Ask for the order

Alternate proposal. This kind of Order-Asking Question seems to be the most common. It simply offers the prospect a choice: "red or blue"; "cash or check"; "the delivery Monday or Tuesday"; and on and on. It offers the prospect a choice of two or more *minor* points.

Minor point. With this close, the salesperson offers but one choice, which is assumed to be the prospect's. "Do you want the red color?" "Do you want us to bill you?" "You are able to see the doctor next Monday, aren't you?"

Impending doom. As ominous as this might sound, this is a perfectly legitimate and proper close in many situations. An impending-doom close uses some time limitation or urgency factor as its basis. If the salesperson is aware of a price increase, this might be said: "We need to get the order in today to avoid the price increase at the beginning of next month." Or, "We've only one unit in stock, and to avoid a waiting period, I had better hold it for you."

Extra inducement. Additional premiums or advantages that might result from an immediate decision by the prospect can be offered as an extra-inducement close. For example: "There is an extra 5 percent discount for cash." "Ordering your installation now will avoid the seasonal rush." Notice, in both situations, you offer the incentive while asking for the order.

The instruction. This close is effective if minor instructions can be given to develop the prospect's mental ownership. By willingly accepting these instructions, the prospect becomes aware the decision has been made. For example: "To get to the doctor's office, turn right on Main Street until you reach the medical center." "You don't want to forget to store your information in your computer before you turn it off!"

Ask for the order. Should you forget to use any of the above and if the order is there, just ask for it. I would dearly love to have the commissions lost in any one day that were there for the asking but not received because a salesperson didn't venture to close. If the prospect has made a buying decision, even a heavy Order-Asking Question will generally not lose the sale. You could say, "You want to pay $175,000 and move in next week, huh?" . . . and probably still get the order! Although it is much better to have the Order-Asking Question "light" in weight, it is better to have asked too heavy a question at the moment of decision than not to have asked at all.

And lastly, but no less importantly, should be our concentration on the *attitude* of the salesperson at the time of closing. "Positive!" is the response of many when asked. Remember, we suggested that *positive* be replaced with *confident,* and it certainly applies in closing. Let's look for a word that might better explain the correct closing attitude.

A more descriptive word that identifies a proper closing attitude is *assumptive.* One should assume not only that the prospect is ready to buy but also that the prospect *has already bought!* Your assumptive behavior helps relax the prospect at the closing's traumatic moment.

Included in the salesperson's actions is the relaxed completion of a few minor details, and perhaps a few major ones, too, that are necessary to execute the order. A professional salesperson needs to be so assumptive because the strength of this attitude reassures the prospect the decision was expected and correct.

Trusting we have now put most of the problems of closing at rest, I am anxiously awaiting the opportunity to address other problems in the sales presentation. Nearly 36 percent of the salespeople in the Salesperson Survey acknowledged closing as their biggest problem. I can rest easier believing I have already solved the greatest concern of over one-third of all my readers!

But, read on ... experience tells me you will undoubtedly discover techniques even more important to you. It is the discovery of the need for improvement in areas of which you are unaware that can be the most satisfying! Besides, I'm saving the most exciting ingredient of the closing procedure until later!

CHAPTER SUMMARY

Before starting the next chapter, please take a moment to answer this question:

What was the one most important idea you received from this chapter, and how are you going to apply it today?

Some of the more important ideas were:

- The secret of closing is not in knowing *how* to ask for the order but in knowing *when* to close!
- The correct time to close the sale is after the customer has already bought!
- Use a Trial Close, asking for an OPINION, to determine the prospect's buying temperature to see whether he or she is cold, warm, or hot toward buying.
- The six words—*"In your opinion, do you feel . . . "*—represent a buying thermometer.
- This instrument helps you to determine precisely WHEN to close.
- Use an Order-Asking Question, asking for a DECISION, only when the prospect has already bought. This appropriate time can be determined with the proper use of Trial Closes.
- Knowing the six ways to ask for the order gives you more versatility in closing.
- Order-Asking Questions should always ask for minor decisions so that a prospect experiences little or no trauma in answering them.

CHAPTER 4

The Steps to a Sale

ONE OF a professional's key attributes in any field is the ability to *analyze*. Salespeople who cannot analyze the various aspects of an interview are doomed to repeat failures and are unable to improve their performance on a day-to-day basis! A professional salesperson should be able to pick a sales presentation apart, bit-by-bit and step-by-step, to identify its strengths and weaknesses. Once able to do this, we build confidence as we look forward to not repeating the same mistakes and consciously to repeating the successful aspects.

The selling interview can be divided into five basic parts. These parts, known as the steps of the sale, are interdependent and consecutive. Each sales interview should be planned in advance to include each step. However, once involved in the interview, all steps may not be required.

THE FIVE STEPS OF A SALE

Conversation
Curiosity
Conviction
Desire
Close

Actually, there are many "sales" within one sale. You need to get a decision in your favor *in each* step. Let's look at the objective of each of the five steps:

Conversation Step: To sell the prospect on yourself and/or your company.

Curiosity Step: To sell the prospect on wanting to listen to you.

Conviction Step: To sell the prospect on the features and benefits of your product.

Desire Step: To sell the prospect on the emotional end result of your proposal.

Closing Step: To sell the prospect on accepting your proposal.

In every sale, a prospect's thinking process works through all five steps *before* buying. However, in some situations, the prospect may not need to be led through each step by the salesperson. It is imperative for a salesperson to know the selling process well enough to ascertain whether or not all the steps are necessary.

For example, if a prospect rushed into your office and said, "I need delivery Monday!" . . . you wouldn't answer, "Wait a minute! I've got four more steps to work through with you first!" In such a situation, it is apparent the prospect had traversed the other steps prior to coming into your office.

In another instance, suppose your prospect asks specific, technical questions about your product. Then, the introductory Conversation Step and the Curiosity Step would be inappropriate since the purpose of each step has already been fulfilled.

Before going into the techniques, subtleties, and sophistication of the selling process, chapter by chapter, let's take an overview of the five steps.

The Conversation Step. The purpose of this step is to sell one's self, and perhaps the company, by establishing rapport. During this step, you establish credibility and trust, and get acquainted as quickly as possible. It is a very normal, natural procedure to relax the prospect early in the interview by engaging in comfortable conversation.

Done properly, at the end of this step, the prospect should be mentally saying, "I like this salesperson and am enjoying this conversation." It would be foolish to proceed in the interview unless the prospect is listening to you and liking you. In the Salesperson Survey, about 10 percent of experienced sales professionals admit needing help in this area.

The Curiosity Step. The purpose of this step is to open the prospect's mind to your presentation. Perhaps the easiest and shortest step of the selling process, it is often overlooked. This step might be seen as a smooth transition between establishing rapport and getting down to business in product presentation. If this step is executed properly, the prospect should be mentally saying, "Tell me more!"

The Conviction Step. The purpose of this step is to convince the prospect of the wisdom of purchasing a product, service, or idea. Features, benefits, and evidence primarily make up this step. The logical part of the sales presentation, this step is vital to effective, convincing communication with the prospect. Most objections arise during this step.

When this step is accomplished successfully, the prospect should be mentally saying, "It is a good product and would benefit me. It is fairly priced, and if I really *want* it, I will be justified in buying it."

The Desire Step. The purposes of this step are threefold:

1. To remind the prospect of a problem, need, or desire.
2. To get the prospect's agreement if it exists.
3. Then, to emotionally disturb, or motivate, the prospect to improve or rectify the situation.

This motivation is accomplished by appealing to the emotional impulses that might cause a prospect to want to buy. This important, somewhat sophisticated procedure of using concrete language is rarely used except by the true professional. Since people buy from emotions and not by logic, awareness and use of the procedures in this step can bring huge dividends.

In the majority of selling situations, prospects take this step on their own. However, a professional salesperson must know when it is necessary to channel the prospect through this step. If this step is done correctly, the prospect should think, "I want it!"

The Closing Step. The purpose of this step is to iron out the details necessary for closing, and to let the prospect become aware that he or she has decided to buy! This step consummates the sale. A professional salesperson recognizes and relies on buying signals to determine when the prospect has arrived at a favorable decision. Once buying signals are evident, all that remains is to accept the order.

Once you understand the purpose of each of these steps, you can determine where you may have failed in an interview *at least 80 percent of the time* by asking yourself one question.

What was the *last* thing the prospect *really* said when emphatically saying "no!"

Let's look at some examples of what prospects might strongly support as a reason for not buying and what you might deduce from their statements:

"I have my own supplier!"

Analysis: The selling of yourself, and your company, is incomplete. Your own credibility is in question. A competitor has apparently done a better job of establishing rapport than you. Before any sale can take place, more concentration is necessary during the Conversation Step to enable you to sell yourself. In fact, it might take several interviews to establish the relationship you need with this prospect.

"I'm not interested!"

Analysis: The prospect is telling you that *you* were not interesting. Probably, your Curiosity Step was not properly planned, nor effectively used. This step should be so well prepared that no prospect could honestly stick by this response.

"I need to shop around!"
"Your price is too high!"
"I prefer your competitor's product!"

Analysis: These remarks, and many others similar in nature, strongly indicate the prospect is not yet convinced. The Conviction Step of your presentation needs more personalized features, benefits and/or evidence. Most rejections, and accompanying loss of sales, occur in this step.

"Sounds good, but I don't want to right now!"

Analysis: The prospect sounds convinced but has other priorities with stronger emotional impact causing hesitancy. The operative word here is *want*. This should have triggered the Desire Step. An effective appeal to the emotions might well have made the sale.

CHAPTER SUMMARY

As you analyze your selling interviews, become especially alert to those unsuccessful situations in which you repeatedly hear the same response from different prospects. If this should happen, adjust your presentation to steer clear of the problem area.

If you can immediately identify a weakness in a particular sales step by this analysis, consider reading the chapter in this book that deals with that step of the sale. It could be exciting to solve a current problem right away!

Think about the importance of learning to differentiate among the steps of the selling process. Please answer this question:

What was the one most important idea you received from this chapter, and how are you going to apply it today?

Some of the important ideas were:

- A professional salesperson should be able to analyze the reasons for the success or failure of each and every presentation.
- Analyzation helps build confidence for the next interview.
- Prospects go through five steps in every successful interview, whether or not you take them through each phase.
- Can you state the purpose of each of the five steps to a sale?
- If one misses a sale, careful analyzation of what the prospect used as an "excuse for not buying" often alerts the salesperson to any weakness in the presentation.

CHAPTER 5

Abolishing Call Reluctance

EVEN THOUGH I know it dates me, when I consider call reluctance, I often think of Elmer Fudd on the old weekly Jack Benny radio show. Posing as a salesperson, Fudd knocks on a prospect's door, mumbling under his breath, "There is nobody in, I hope, I hope, I hope!" Breathes there a salesperson who doesn't understand the feeling?

Have you ever experienced call reluctance? Do you remember forcing yourself to make calls simply because it was your job? Has it happened recently?

Anyone who has spent any time in the selling profession knows this feeling of apprehension very well. It can be an agonizing experience, especially for the newer salesperson. Untreated, repeated call reluctance is responsible for much costly turnover of sales personnel. It can even rob the experienced salesperson of enthusiasm and self-esteem.

Review the definition of "the professional." The professional is one who thinks in terms of the client's interest—*first, last,* and *always.* Salespeople who experience call reluctance can only be thinking about *themselves*—first, last, and always. In short, call reluctance is *unprofessional!* Herein lies the principal cause of this affliction!

Understanding the source of call reluctance is only *symptomatic.* It does not cure the ill. To do this, we must identify specific ways to get in tune with our prospects by concentrating our thoughts and concerns about *them*. Doing this takes our minds off ourselves. Freeing yourself of call reluctance requires a conscious effort in preparing for each call. If *you really knew* that as a direct result of your next call your prospect's life would be happier and *your sale would be successful*, then call reluctance would be nonexistent!

What conscious procedure can a salesperson take to remove thoughts of self from prominence, and transfer concern to the prospect? This can be accomplished by doing a better job of *fact-finding* prior to the call! Fact-finding is the gathering of pertinent information about the prospect to enable the salesperson to justify the purchase of the salesperson's product, idea, or service.

Because a sophisticated salesperson is fact-finding all the time, it is not a separate step of the sale. The most common time for fact-finding is before the interview. However, an alert salesperson is constantly fact-finding during an interview, and translating the information learned into useful features and benefits. Also, if one expects repeat business from the prospect, additional information may be uncovered after the interview for use in future sales.

Fact-finding has other names of identification in our profession. Many call it *preapproach*. Some refer to it simply as *qualifying the prospect*. In my program, I often refer to it as *blueprinting the prospect*. Regardless of its name, this important role of the professional demands a deep understanding of, and empathy with, the client.

Hundreds of questions could be asked and a wide range of information could be useful to you in fact-finding. Perhaps it is this sense of enormity that keeps too many salespeople from asking *any* fact-finding questions at all. Certainly, some specific questions related exclusively to your own product or service would be inapplicable for salespeople in other fields.But, we can organize this potentially vast data bank and make gathering of the information simple by separating the fact-finding process into only five general categories:

Needs
Wants
Authority
Capital
Dominant buying motive

In preparing for an interview, you can begin to acquire the professional objectivity necessary to help your prospect by reviewing these five categories. Thinking of your prospect—first, last, and always—ask yourself if you know the answers to the following questions:

Needs. Does your prospect recognize his or her real need for your product or service? If not, what preparation is necessary for your interview to alert your client to the importance of these needs? The professional salesperson can often be more realistic and objective concerning the urgency of these needs than the client. For example, a prospect may *need* a three-bedroom home to accommodate the size of the family; or a prospect may *need* fuel economy because of the rising cost of gas.

Before and during your presentation, it is your responsibility to analyze how best your prospect could personally benefit by your proposal. What situations exist that cause you to be enthusiastic about your recommendations? You'll look forward to the call if real enthusiasm exists.

Wants. Occasionally, a prospect's needs and wants are the same. More often, however, they are not. What are your prospect's priorities? Many times you'll find a prospect's tendency will be to invest in what he or she *wants* rather than in what you may know the prospect *needs*. Sometimes, you will professionally think this unwise. Your objectivity may be very important. For example, a prospect may *want* a luxurious home that exceeds the budget, or may *want* a gas-guzzler because it gives a smoother ride.

To avoid challenging a prospect's beliefs, you will not want to point out a thinking error, but you must be aware if a disparity between needs and wants exists. In the fact-finding stage, perceptive questioning is important to help you really get a feel for your prospect's viewpoints.

Don't minimize the importance of wants, because they, too, can lead to the sale. After all, it is the prospect who must make the final decision, and we may be required to provide exactly what he or she wants.

Just suppose for the moment you know what your prospect *needs* and *wants*. And suppose you know your product would supply the benefits to satisfy the situation. How would you feel about the call? What would happen to call reluctance?

Authority. Who has the authority to buy from you? Does it make any sense to attempt to sell to someone who cannot make a final decision? If you blunder into an interview without this information, you waste both your time and your prospect's. This is a key fact-finding question that needs answering.

You can get this information before an interview in many ways. Call ahead and ask the receptionist or secretary about the potential client's title. Check available information about the company's officers through various publications. Sometimes, even your prospect's competitors can provide insight as to whom you should contact. Whatever means you use to find the one individual with the authority to make the decision, it will be time well spent!

Nothing is more frustrating than to complete a presentation and be told that someone else will have to make the decision. If early in the interview you sense you may have called on the wrong person, simply ask: "Were a decision to be made, you do have the authority to make it, don't you?"

If the answer is a "no!" then ask to be introduced to the right person. You, having made the mistake, should extend the courtesy for this individual to accompany you during your presentation to the one in authority. Offering this keeps you from embarrassing your first contact.

Capital. Can the prospect afford your product? Does the company have the budget required? A well-prepared salesperson takes the time and effort to ascertain the answers to these questions prior to the call. Knowing in advance that money is not a problem will insulate you from the I-can't-afford-it defense commonly used. In the long run, it saves a lot of time and frustration, especially if you know the capital required for purchase is not a problem.

Just suppose, for the moment, you know your prospect's needs and wants. You know the capital is readily available, and your appointment is with the person responsible to make the final decision! Could you possibly have call reluctance under these conditions?

Fact-finding in the categories of needs, wants, authority, and capital provides objective, logical information. This information, on its own, will not always lead you to a sale. Ask any group of salespeople whether people buy from emotion or by logic, and the unanimous answer will be "emotion!" The previous four categories of fact-finding questions are *very logical* considerations in gathering information about a prospect.

Therefore, we need to go deeper into the emotional considerations that influence the buying decision. Understanding a prospect's dominant buying motive, and the emotional aspects it represents, will put you head and shoulders ahead of your competition and make selling easier and more profitable.

Dominant buying motive. What is the dominant buying motive, or DBM, that will cause the prospect to buy? What are the prospect's dreams, desires, and longings? How could what you have to offer fulfill those dreams?

To understand this critical aspect of fact-finding, we must define terms:

> *dominant* = ruling, controlling, principle, #1
> *buying* = purchasing, acquiring, gaining
> *motive* = impulse, driving force, stimulus

Putting these three words together, you have

dominant buying motive = #1 *purchasing impulse* that *causes* a prospect to buy!

Just how important can this particular element of fact-finding be? If you know a prospect's dominant buying motive, the sale is 70 percent over because this is what *causes a prospect to buy!* Strangely enough, this "driving force" is overlooked by almost all salespeople in their presentations. They think that if they pile on enough facts, the prospect is certain to buy from the force of sheer logic.

What does a dominant buying motive look like? It can be described most simply as the mental image a prospect has when using, enjoying, and benefiting from the purchase of the product or service. If you can visualize this in your mind's eye exactly as the prospect might see it, you have the key to the sale!

Get a significant insight into the dominant buying motive with questions such as, "Were you to invest in a product like this, what would you most enjoy about owning it?" Listen carefully to the answer, and it might open the door to *why* the prospect might buy from you! If your questions could elicit a description of what in his or her mind would be enjoyable circumstances of the end use of your product, then you draw even closer to the motivating force that could cause a purchase.

Once you identify the DBM, your responsibility is to cause the mental image to be seen in the mind's eye of the prospect. Once the prospect shares this mental picture, you are on the way to a successful sale. Always remember: Prospects buy from emotions, not by logic!

Why do you suppose automobile salespeople are so anxious to get you into their cars for a demonstration ride? It is because they have learned from experience that when the prospect feels the comfort of the ride, smells the newness of the car, hears the quietness of the motor, sees the color and design of the interior, and senses the power of the engine . . . emotions take over, and prospects envision the trips they plan to take, or dominant buying motive! A truly professional salesperson would ask questions about these trips, helping the prospect to project future enjoyment.

We will learn how to create this emotional force when we focus on the fourth step of the sale, the Desire Step, in Chapter 13. For the moment, devote more time to your fact-finding and look for the dominant buying motive. Concentrate on benefits, which are sometimes emotional, rather than on product features, which are always logical.

For example, if the end result of your product could possibly lead to a promotion of your client, discuss the pleasant activities of the new position. Should your prospect save money in purchasing from you, talk about what he or she might do with the savings. If your product or service should make your prospect's job easier, review the day-to-day conveniences of using your product.

Analyzing three of the five categories of fact-finding, take careful note that the *needs* and the *wants* deal with *what* a prospect might need or want. The *dominant buying motive* deals with *why* a prospect might want the product.

And now for the most important question I can ask in this chapter. Just suppose, for the moment, you know your prospect's needs; you know what the prospect wants; you know he or she has the authority to make the decision and the capital to invest. And, you know the prospect's dreams, or desires, and how you could satisfy those dreams if your product is purchased. How *would you feel* about making a call on this prospect? Call reluctance could not possibly bother you, could it? *You can eliminate call reluctance by doing a competent job of fact-finding.*

When defined and thoroughly understood, most technical terms used in the selling profession help us to communicate more precisely. One term that is harmful, however, is *cold calls*. This term usually denotes either new or inactive accounts. I have actually seen it strike fear in the hearts of salespeople. Why should any call be *cold*? The word causes a salesperson to resist making the call. With the prior fact-finding, one should look forward to the interview rather than dread it. This changes the *cold call* to a *hot knock!* Let's do our part in eliminating the use of this term altogether!

In a magazine some years ago, I was fascinated by an article contributed by an investment executive, Robert Cruikshank. He emphasized the need for fact-finding by stating that the *only* two reasons prospects don't buy are:

1. They are unaware of their problem.
2. They are not sufficiently disturbed by it.

Therefore, he stated, it is the salesperson's responsibility during interviews to make prospects aware of their problem and sufficiently disturb them about it. This seemingly innocuous admonition needs to be read and reread. This problem of the prospects is really what we are searching for in our fact-finding. Finding prospects' problems and solving them are the pathway to the sale!

Could it be that this chapter offers the solution to what 8 percent of management in the Sales Management Survey consider to be the #1 problem of their salespeople? Certainly, call reluctance can be costly, and painful. It is hoped you have found an inexpensive antidote.

CHAPTER SUMMARY

Take a moment to answer this question:

What was the one most important idea you received from this chapter, and how are you going to apply it today?

Some of the highlights of this chapter were:

- A professional salesperson thinks in terms of the client's interest—first, last, and always. If you experience call reluctance, you must be thinking of *yourself and are, therefore, unprofessional!*
- Fact-finding is the gathering of pertinent information about the prospect that will enable the salesperson to justify the purchase of the product, idea, or service.
- Fact-finding is not a step of the sale. A professional is constantly fact-finding and translating the information into useful features and benefits.
- It is a simple process to fact-find if one separates the process into five general categories:

Needs
Wants
Authority
Capital
Dominant buying motive

- If a salesperson truly knows a prospect's dominant buying motive, the sale is 70 percent over!

Proper fact-finding eliminates call reluctance!

CHAPTER 6

The Conversation Step

Now for a trick question! How many chances do you get to make a favorable first impression? If your answer is "one," it is incorrect.

Perhaps two personal examples might give you a clue as to the truth about first impressions.

When I was a sales engineer for a heating distributor in Milwaukee, Wisconsin, in the early fifties, I called on about 150 heating dealers. Many of my calls were made weekly, and I can still hear some of my customers saying, "Are you here again?" or, "Is it Tuesday again?" I felt like a real nuisance and often wanted to crawl into a hole.

Then, I got an idea! Every Saturday, back at the warehouse, I sorted through our thousands of products and took one with me the following week on every call. Some were heavy castings, and not too pleasant to haul out of my car when I was dressed in a suit, crisp white shirt, and tie. As I walked into a dealership, I began to hear, "Lee, I didn't know you stocked that. I just gave a gross order for those to Auer Steel last week." Can you imagine how that made me feel?

On the other hand, many times I received orders I would not have gotten without this little bit of special effort. More importantly, my dealers tended to look forward to my calls because I sometimes reminded them of something they needed or of something they wanted to know. I no longer felt I was imposing upon my prospects' time.

53

How many chances do you get to make a favorable first impression? We make either a good or a bad "first impression" *each* and *every* time we call upon a prospect. The idea to carry a different product on each call was my first realization that I needed a different beginning for each repetitive call. I was trying to earn respect as something other than "just a peddler." I no longer needed to hang my head and worry about being an intruder in the busy work schedule of my customers because I had something to offer that was important to their business.

I also remember calling upon Stan's Heating Service on my very first week with the company. I was shocked when Stan greeted me: "Look! There is absolutely no reason for you to stop here. I give all of my business to Auer Steel because I don't like your company. I have had too much trouble with your boss in the past. Besides, your service is lousy!"

Although I certainly wasn't expecting this tirade, I recovered enough to reply, "I'm sorry you have had bad experiences with us. I do admire your loyalty to my competitor and wouldn't expect you to change and do business with me immediately. But I would like to continue to drop by each Monday morning for a very brief visit. Someday I may be able to help you in a situation in which Auer Steel cannot. Perhaps then I might personally follow through and rectify the kind of service you have had with us in the past."

It took eight or nine months of weekly five-minute visits before he gave me my first order. In effect, it took that long to make a favorable first impression with Stan. It would have been useless to attempt to "sell" him anything until my creditability was established. Stan's Heating Service later became one of my best accounts. Several years later, while taking a sales course, I properly cataloged in my mind what I had intuitively done!

How carefully do you plan to make a good first impression on each interview? Do you think about what you are going to say in the Conversation Step? Or, are you going to blunder in like Elmer Fudd saying, "There is nobody in, I hope, I hope, I hope!"

The first two steps of the sale should be carefully planned before each and every interview. These two steps are the Conversation Step, in which you sell yourself, and the Curiosity Step, where you sell the prospect on wanting to hear your presentation (see Chapter 7).

Preplanning will never be wasted effort, since it heightens your awareness to the need for a good beginning at each interview! At times, even though you have planned what you will say, circumstances may occur during the opening minutes of your sales call that give you an opportunity to improve upon what you had planned. The first few minutes of an interview can possibly determine the success or failure of your sales presentation.

The *purpose* of the Conversation Step is to get the prospect to *listen* to you and to *like* you. Establishing a good rapport enhances your own credibility. It should be done in a relaxed, conversational manner and with a pleasant smile on your face. Greet your prospect as you would greet a close friend whom you haven't seen for some time. Remember, you are selling *yourself,* not your product, in this vital step.

Many methods can make a good first impression. Let's list some of them:

A compliment
Questions bearing on needs, wants, or
dominant buying motive
Use of referrals
A gift
Mutual interests
Say a big name

Story-type examples
Service opener
Curiosity opener
Exhibit

Consider the following explanations of the different professional methods by which you can establish rapport in the Conversation Step. Identify which of the procedures you have used most often in the past and the ones you might wish to use effectively in the future.

The compliment. One of the best ways to get into comfortable conversation is by paying a compliment. Don't confuse compliments with flattery. By definition, a compliment offers sincere praise. Flattery, on the other hand, does not, and can get a salesperson seeking to establish a good first impression off to a shaky start.

Salespeople often avoid compliments because of a concern about flattery. Learning how to pay compliments can help to avoid this. First, let's identify three kinds of compliments that can enable you to improve your complimenting skills:

A direct compliment

An indirect compliment

A quoted compliment

As the term implies, a *direct* compliment is generated by the complimenter and paid directly to the person. For example: "Mr. Jones, I understand that your division led the company in sales last year. That is certainly a credit to you as the manager!"

An *indirect* compliment refers to one you may have previously dropped to your prospect's associate. Although not used in your interview, it may have preceded you. If you are in the habit of paying compliments, sometimes you can create a good first impression by having them passed on indirectly.

A *quoted* compliment is perhaps the most effective compliment you can use. You are instantly believed when you are thoughtful enough to repeat a compliment you heard about your prospect! The fact you had to remember the details of the quoted compliment assures you it will be considered as sincere. Ultimately, you might make two friends with a quoted compliment. One friend is the person you quote; the other is the person to whom you convey the compliment.

Here are some simple rules to follow in complimenting that will assure you of the best results:

1. Avoid complimenting the obvious. Be discerning enough to select your compliments about items that are not too readily seen. The prospect with a bowling trophy on the desk has probably heard lots of comments about it. Find something more remarkable.

2. Try to compliment the person's *action* rather than appearance. For example, a prospect might be unmoved about comments on their manner of dress but very appreciative when hearing a compliment regarding a recent speech at the Lions Club. (We are never so confident about the things we do as we are about our appearance.)

3. To be absolutely sure your compliment has a sincere ring, NEVER tell a person *what* you like unless you tell them *why* you like it! For example: Don't say, "I like your office!" Instead say, "I certainly am impressed with the choice of colors in your office. The wall colors go well with the furniture and seem to make the room bigger. Did you pick them out yourself?"

These three simple rules will guide you in effectively using compliments in the Conversation Step. This is an easy way to get into comfortable, relaxed conversation, and can encourage the prospect to listen to you and like you almost instantly.

Questions bearing on needs, wants, or dominant buying motive. Starting your interview with fact-finding questions can be an excellent way to get into a comfortable conversation. In this case, your fact-finding questions also serve as the Conversation Step. For example, you make a good first impression anytime at the beginning of the interview by asking questions pertaining to needs, wants, or dominant buying motives. People like to talk about themselves.

If you find prospects willing to talk about themselves, ask enough questions to encourage them. Listen attentively to what they have to say. Getting prospects to talk early will guarantee that prospects will listen to you later. Let the Law of Psychological Reciprocity and the Law of Challenging Belief work for you!

The referral. I personally believe that using a referral is the most effective way to establish rapport early in the interview. After many years in the sales training business, I have earned the luxury of many referral sources and now use this more than any other kind of opening. Years of experience can do the same for you!

It is very effective to use a referral when you know that your prospect has a mutual respect for the person recommending you or your product. Simply begin the interview by talking about your common acquaintance. Combine this with a quoted compliment you were given by the referral, and you have instant credibility. If possible, tell your prospect how your mutual acquaintance profited from the use of your product or service.

A gift. Years ago, Fuller Brush salespeople always gave away a small brush as a gift when the client answered the knock at the door. This was a natural entrée to their discussion about brushes and other Fuller Brush products.

A sample, brochure, or advertising gift, such as notepads with your company's logo, can be an effective "door opener" when you first greet your prospect. In some cases, this can be a good way to start into comfortable conversation.

Mutual interests. Opening the sales interview by talking about items of mutual interest can help you to become an interesting conversationalist. Should you know your prospect is an avid baseball fan, and you share this enthusiasm, then talk about the leagues' standings. Art, avocations, music, hobbies, and many other topics of mutual interest can serve as sources of interesting discussion.

WARNING! Be absolutely certain that your interests are *mutual* if you are to use this approach. Feigning interest in another's pastimes or hobbies can be instantly perceived as contrived. If this occurs, your efforts may backfire on you.

Say a big name. Some people like to talk about important personages. Should you know something newsworthy about a giant in your industry, a conversation can be started with this phrase: "Did you hear about? . . . "

Although risky, "name-dropping" of an important, mutual acquaintance can sometimes be effective in getting into conversation.

Story-type examples. Some salespeople are good story-tellers. A story about an interesting or humorous incident in your industry can start a good relationship with a prospect. Also, a success story of someone in your field can be an effective conversation opener.

If jokes are used, off-color ones are not suggested. They can offend too easily. Be certain, though, that you and your prospect share a sense of humor. If this happens to be the case, you can brighten the day for many with the use of humor and, at the same time, help the prospect listen to you and like you.

Service opener. Are you required to make some service calls as well as sales calls? Many salespeople do not realize that when performing service work for a client, they might already be in the Conversation Step of the sale.

For example, servicing or repairing an old unit can establish excellent rapport with clients. Their gratitude often "opens the door" to further discussion of newer models or expanded service opportunities.

Curiosity opener. With a little imagination, you can plan your opening conversation with your prospect to plant seeds of curiosity about your call. You purposely do this to establish a bridge smoothly into the Curiosity Step and start your presentation on the right track more quickly (see Chapter 7).

Prepare your opening questions in the Conversation Step to open your prospect's mind to the Curiosity Step, which follows. Think for the moment of your product's newest features and complete this question: "Have you heard that? . . ."

For example: When selling sales training to a general agent of an insurance company, I might ask, "Have you heard that the National Association of Life Underwriters estimates it takes $150,000 to get a salesperson into production?" Any manager facing the high cost of doing business will be curious about what I might say after that!

Exhibit. Earlier I mentioned carrying different products on each weekly sales call. Actually, I was using exhibits to initiate conversations with my heating dealers and to vary my approach. The more unusual the exhibit, the more readily questions developed that caused my prospect to want to listen to me! Once a good rapport was established, I was free to discuss any number of items in my complete product line.

Although I've had many salespeople tell me they prefer to sell "bare-handed," I've wondered if they understand the power of an exhibit as a conversation piece. Do you have a product that lends itself to this form of opener?

Now that we have identified and discussed a variety of ways to professionally start an interview in the Conversation Step of the sale, follow this admonition!

Don't stay in the Conversation Step too long.

How long is too long? It is that point at which you become a conversationalist and not a salesperson. It is that moment when you impose yourself unnecessarily upon the prospect's valuable time with trite commentary. It is that time when you forget about the purpose of this step! It is a situation in which you can easily lose control of the interview by talking too much.

"How long should this step be?" you might ask. It should last until you are reasonably sure that you have sold yourself. It should last until the prospect listens to you and likes you. It may take a minute, five minutes, or, in some unusual cases, it might take several calls!

Have you ever wondered how tiring it must be for purchasing agents to talk repetitiously about the weather as they greet salespeople calling on them? Since it is one of their responsibilities to interview dozens of company sales representatives each week, it would be interesting to learn what percentage of these sales calls are feebly started with such trite conversations.

Are you now prepared to use a more diverse approach with your prospects? From this moment on, resolve to plan your opening remarks more carefully. Such planning should ultimately help you to establish rapport more quickly and shorten the time of your interviews.

CHAPTER SUMMARY

Think about what you learned in the Conversation Step and answer this question:

What was the one most important idea you received from this chapter, and how are you going to apply it today?

Key discoveries about this step might include:

- Each time you call on a prospect you make a "first impression."
- A professional salesperson should carefully think through the first two steps of the sale immediately prior to each interview.

- The purpose of the Conversation Step is to get the prospect to *listen* to you and *like* you.

- Make a good first impression by varying your approach. Can you name the *ten* different ways to be a sparkling conversationalist mentioned in this chapter?

- Get into the habit of complimenting people in *three* different ways: (1) direct, (2) indirect, or (3) quoted.

- Don't stay in the Conversation Step too long.

CHAPTER 7

The Curiosity Step

"I'M NOT interested!" Perhaps those three words have defeated more salespeople than any others in the English language. One can only dream of the millions of dollars in commissions that might have been earned had the sales representative only known that with very little effort the prospect could have become interested. More importantly, in those same situations, the salesperson could have had a happy, satisfied customer!

It sometimes seems when salespeople hear those words, they "fold their tents and steal away." Look at their faces! All but the most stoic betray defeat and dissolution. Many seem to take it as a rejection of their product . . . others take it personally. Some just seem to be confused as to why it happened. Several consider it time for a cup of coffee, or something stronger, and catch a very serious, sometimes fatal, disease called the Shufflin' Blues. This means, rather than making another call, they shuffle through their remaining prospect cards muttering, "He's no good . . . She's not really a prospect . . . This is the wrong day to call on them!" Sometimes the next call is terribly hard to make.

What kind of assumption do you make when you hear, "I'm not interested!" Do you always take prospects at their word or do you rationalize? Can we afford to rationalize that our timing was wrong, our idea was wrong, or our poor prospect really didn't have the money? When you hear, "I'm not interested," are you absolutely certain you have a full understanding of why a prospect says this to you?

Remember Cruikshank's statement of the two reasons prospects don't buy: Either they are unaware of their problem, or, they are not sufficiently disturbed by it. Could it be that we could arouse curiosity by taking these words to heart right now?

When you point a finger at someone, remember, there are three fingers pointing back at you! The main reason prospects are "not interested!" *is because we are not interesting.* From this point on, the three words "I'm not interested!" should trigger a reaction within you of a three-word question: "Was I interesting?"

It would be far better to prepare your Curiosity Step so well that the prospect could not honestly confront you with disinterest. Reviewing Chapter 4, it is stated that this is the step in which you *sell* the prospect on *wanting* to listen to you. This is the step, if executed properly, when the prospect should be mentally saying, "Tell me more!"

The Curiosity Step is *so* easy because it is usually only one sentence long. The benefit to you in learning to use this important sentence is it can virtually eliminate lack of interest or a premature negative reaction. The real benefit to you will be the satisfaction resulting from increased sales! Here is the rule:

RULE FOR AROUSING CURIOSITY

**Arouse your prospect's curiosity by *stating* a big, fat claim, bearing upon needs, wants, dominant buying motive *providing you can prove it later on.*

I'll not apologize for calling this a rule, knowing as I do that often salespeople don't feel they need rules. I must disagree. Rules are almost as important as the Law of Psychological Reciprocity and the Law of Challenging Belief. Rules help to give you an understanding of good selling procedure, and also help you to formulate more effective and persuasive words in your sales presentation.

Now, let us analyze the Rule for Arousing Curiosity. We will concentrate on some of the more important words in the rule, and discuss the rule's use:

Stating. Many feel you arouse curiosity by asking questions. You *arouse curiosity* most forcefully with a *statement*, not by asking questions as you do in the Conversation Step to get into comfortable conversation (see Chapter 5).

Big, fat claim. When does a claim become a fact? In the selling vernacular, a claim does not become a fact until the prospect *accepts* it as a fact. (Later we will differentiate between a *big, fat claim* and a *little, fat claim.*) A big, fat claim is about the merits of *all* of the features and benefits of the *entire* presentation. Your big, fat claim should be so interesting that the prospect should be curious enough to think or say, "Tell me about it!"

Prove it. Be aware once you have *proven* your claim, interest is satisfied. The prospect will no longer be curious once your claims are proven. Salespeople *prove* their claims in the Conviction Step (see Chapter 8).

The following examples illustrate this rule and should help you develop big, fat claims of your own. Curiosity is intensified when claims are personalized with the word *you*. Each claim should have at least two *you*'s:

"We have an idea that might increase your profits and make your job easier."

"We have an idea that might enable your secretary to get your letters done in nearly half the time, and enhance your finished product."

"We have an automobile that will give you greater economy and, at the same time, give you the prestige you deserve."

"We have a program designed to increase the productivity in your company as it eases your work load."

"We have a plan that might ensure an earlier retirement for you while, at the same time, provide you with the money to live in luxury in Hawaii."

Note the more personalized last example. The more you know about your prospect before the interview, the more interesting your big, fat claim can be. The less you know about the prospect, the more generalized, and less interesting, your claim will be.

As I read back over these examples of big, fat claims, I can't get over the feeling that they lack punch. The reason is I do not have specific prospects in mind and, therefore, do not have fact-finding information to make them more appealing. However, you will find when a "live" prospect is considered, and your sentence is designed to appeal directly to the individual, the effect can be powerful!

Does it sound impractical to spend an entire chapter on what amounts to not more than one or two sentences of your presentation? The Curiosity Step of the sale is *skipped* by more salespeople than any other step. If I thought it would do any good, I would enlarge the coverage of this topic by two or three chapters. It is unbelievable to me that some salespeople disregard the importance of this step even after learning about it. May this not happen to you.

Time now for introspection! How much time have you spent in the past in mental preparation, personalizing your opening remarks so that your prospect wants to listen to you? It is just as easy as it would be to prepare the first sentence of a display ad for a newspaper or magazine.

Think how carefully you might design the first sentence of a large display advertisement in the newspaper. I am told at least 60 to 70 percent of one's time is spent preparing the eye-catching heading to the ad. When advertisers are asked why it is so time-consuming, they reply, "Because I want the reader's *attention!*"

Study the response. It is incorrect! People who happen to see an ad have their *attention* riveted on the newspaper. The purpose of the opening line is to arouse their *curiosity* so that they will want to read the *rest of the ad*. It is very important to draw a distinction between *attention* and *curiosity* to enable you to understand this difference in a sales interview.

Let us compare the disparity between attention and interest in an advertisement to its parallel within a sales presentation. In the Conversation Step, you want the *attention* of the prospect so that he or she will listen to you and like you. In the Curiosity Step, you want to arouse the *curiosity* of the prospect so that he or she will want to hear *the rest of the sales presentation!* These are two separate, distinct functions.

It has always been a singular mystery to me why salespeople, who sometimes prepare display ads, instinctively spend 70 percent of their time on the curiosity sentence in the ad but not one moment thinking about some form of curiosity opener in a sales presentation. Is it because of a dangerous assumption that they think interest has been aroused just because the prospect graciously engages in conversation? Why take such a chance?

Think about the next prospect you intend to see. Reflect on the background information you have about this person. Recall some of your successful interviews with other customers whose circumstances were similar. Decide what motivated them to buy from you. Carefully complete the big, fat claim below in general, persuasive words.

"We have an idea (program, product, service) that will . . ."

Check your work.

Did you use at least two *you*'s? Does the big, fat claim bear upon the needs, wants, and/or dominant buying motive of this particular prospect? Can you prove your claim later in your sales talk?

Are you certain it is so powerful the prospect couldn't honestly say, "I'm not interested!" after hearing it?

Use the above exercise for preplanning each and every call until it becomes habitual. This is certain to make a marked improvement in your sales presentations.

Mastering the ability to use the Conversation Step and the Curiosity Step successfully is only part of the learning process. Equally important is your competence in making a smooth transition between the steps of the sale. To accomplish this, we need to learn another technical term in selling called a *bridge*.

A bridge is a connecting phrase between two different portions, or functions, of the sales interview. Bridges enable you to gather your thoughts and provide continuity even as you speak. Use of bridges will help the prospect follow your reasoning more readily. An important additional benefit is that bridges help you to be more concise!

You have a choice between two excellent bridges that will smoothly connect the Conversation Step to the Curiosity Step. You might regard these bridges as a way of "changing the subject" in your presentation from interesting conversation to starting to get down to business by arousing curiosity. Either bridge will accomplish this:

. . . the reason I mention this, we have a . . . for you
or . . . my purpose is . . .

A bridge between the Curiosity Step and the Conviction Step (see Chapter 8) is:

. . . the name of my product, or program, is . . .

For example:

CONVERSATION STEP (referral): "The other day your friend Ted Larkin told me a little about your struggles to put aside money for a college fund for your children. He suggested I outline what we have done for his family in this regard."

". . . The reason I mention this, we have a . . .

CURIOSITY STEP: ". . . unique investment idea that assures *you* that college tuition costs will be met and, at the same time, can reduce *your* anxieties about future financial strain for *your* children's college needs."

"It is our Education Reserve Plan!"

Another example:

CONVERSATION STEP (compliment): "Mr. Simms, you certainly maintain wonderful store window displays. Each time I visit you I'm impressed with the attention you give to highlighting profitable items, and notice the store traffic it produces!"

". . . My purpose . . ."

CURIOSITY STEP: ". . . for calling upon you today *is* to introduce a new big-ticket item *you* will find highly profitable, and perhaps will increase *your* floor traffic as a window display."

"The name of my product is our energy-efficient air conditioner!"

Now, let's put this together in more conversational style so that you can read how smoothly the two steps can flow together in opening remarks to a prospect:

"Mrs. Jones, when I was in your Houston office last week, I

was told your agency led the company last year in sales. Congratulations!"

"The reason I mention this, we have a

program for successful salespeople like *you*, which complements their skills, increases their sales, and helps *you* maintain *your* prestigious position in the coming years."

"This program is known as "The Lee DuBois Course in Selling Techniques."

For brevity, in these examples, I use only one or two sentences in the Conversation Step. In actual situations, this step would probably be longer. Notice, though, how the bridges help the flow of the presentation move from step to step.

Notice, also, there are at least two *you*'s in each Curiosity Step. The use of two *you*'s is very important to increase your prospect's curiosity and to personalize your interview!

Now, it is time for you to prepare the first two steps of the sale using these important bridges. It will be much easier for you if you have a future prospect in mind. Choose one of the ten ways to get into comfortable conversation, and select which bridge you will use to move into the Curiosity Step. Be certain there are at least two *you*'s in your curiosity statement. Lastly, identify the product or idea you intend to sell:

CONVERSATION STEP

**... the reason I mention this, we have a ... for you
or ... my purpose is ...**

... the name of my product is ...

WARNING! Other than as noted, please do not change the time-tested bridges until you have tried them at least 25 times! Based on experience, I have seen far too many salespeople change the wording too quickly and thereby lose their effectiveness. Sometimes the changing of just one word can do harm. Remember, you will use your own words before and after the bridges, which will express your own feelings and conviction. After 25 times, these bridges probably will become very comfortable for you *and* will become habitual!

A very natural exception to the rule about the changing of bridges is when you are asking *questions* bearing upon needs, wants, or dominant buying motive as part of your Conversation Step. Then, you may find it more comfortable to say, *"The reason I asked those questions is we have a . . . for you!"*

The alternative bridge, *". . . my purpose is . . ."*, was developed almost by accident as a result of training my own salespeople to sell sales training to top management executives. Several days would be spent in role-playing with each new sales representative before the actual sales calls were made. Then, appointments would be made and I would accompany my new sales representative on the interview. It was standard procedure for the new salesperson to conduct the interview while I listened. The trainee was told there would be a critique right after we left the prospect.

Upon arriving in the parking lot at the prospect's place of business, I often startled my new trainees with an innocent question I was accustomed to asking myself before calling upon a prospect. I would say:

"What is the *purpose* of this call?"

Generally, the look I received would be of near disbelief. The trainee must have thought the answer to be very self-evident! "The purpose is to sell sales training" would be the usual answer.

"Such a purpose is of no advantage to the prospect," I would counter. I then added, "I will not make this call with you unless you can give me a reason why this busy executive should listen to you *whether or not* a sale is made!"

Reflecting back on this discussion, I realize this must have seemed like torture to this newly hired salesperson anxious to get this first call completed. However, the discipline involved in this unusual self-examination accelerates the learning process in achieving a successful sales interview, and can help the salesperson to be more interesting!

I would then take a moment to explain the TWO important purposes that should be incorporated in each and every sales call.

1. The advantage for the prospects to listen *whether or not* they buy from us.
2. Our advantage, should we have the opportunity to explain our proposal.

I would explain that both of these purposes should be articulated "up front" in the interview as part of the Curiosity Step. To emphasize this principle, I then asked my new salesperson to use the bridge *". . . my purpose is . . ."* rather than *". . . the reason I mention this . . ."*

For example, bridging from the Conversation Step:

"President Jones, . . . *my purpose* for being here *is* to give you some ideas you can take to your sales force today and increase sales, and, at the same time, tell you about how we might be able to help increase your sales through your utilization of our professional sales training program!"

Not only do the prospects hear interesting reasons to learn about your proposal, but a new dimension is being added that goes beyond the normal interview! It can set you apart from the average salesperson. That dimension is to offer fresh new ideas that may be beneficial to them *whether or not they buy from you*. It, in effect, makes two purposes for each call and promises to make your presentations much more interesting.

My new sales representatives soon discovered how important it was to refocus on the purpose minutes before the interview. Each time it became easier to get down to business in the interview, and to the surprise of the trainees, they were quickly accepted as an authority in their profession.

Implicit in this additional purpose is the fact we were going to give the prospect something for free! This extra inducement for listening should be designed to be well worth the prospect's investment of time during the interview. Before making each call, our trainees learned to decide which sales technique, or sales training idea, they intended to give away. After all, we have dozens of good ideas, so why not be generous and make it financially worthwhile for the executive we call upon to see us?

Furthermore, this somewhat novel approach helped to enhance the salesperson's conviction that he or she is doing a favor for the prospect by calling, rather than feeling the prospect was granting the favor of the interview. This additional purpose is another way to dispel call reluctance.

After several years of training my own salespeople to use ". . . *my purpose is* . . .", I began to mention this bridge to my general sales classes. I found that they liked the bridge, and tended to use it more often than ". . . *the reason I mention this* . . ." bridge. So now, I challenge you to try it! Get in the habit of using it in every interview. Take some time before each call to think of an idea you can "give for free" that would make the time granted in your interview profitable for your prospect. Then, include this idea in the purpose of your call!

At first, you may find this extra purpose rather difficult to conceive. With a little concentration, you will discover you have dozens of ideas to give away, too! With your experience in your field, surely your prospects could profit by your informing them of a new development or of a sales promotion idea. Perhaps they could benefit in other ways from your experience, or your company's experience, which could be imparted within the purpose of your call making it well worth the prospect's time to listen to you! Use your creative imagination so that you will never be categorized as "just another salesperson."

If you make repetitive calls, imagine the respect you will earn from your customer when you have a new idea to give him or her on each call. I'll admit at times it will take some deep thinking, but your professional image will grow with each interview. Competition won't be able to touch you!

Whether or not you have properly prepared what to say in your sales presentation, you will find this bridge will force you to be more succinct and much more interesting. *"My purpose is . . ."* gives you a direction to go in the interview. At the same time, it lets the prospect know what you hope to accomplish and what are their advantages in listening·to you.

Perhaps you will feel like Don Nidey, agent for the Equitable Life Insurance Company of Iowa, who wrote after completing my sales training program, "I firmly believe that the best idea I received was *'. . . my purpose is . . .'* Lee, I really believe this one phrase is the key that I had been looking and searching for."

Take, for example, my own experience using this technique.

My prospect came out of his office, stood by the receptionist's desk, and growled, "What do *you* want?"

I remember using a very brief compliment and stating, *"My purpose for being here is* to give you some ideas you can immediately take to your salespeople and increase sales. Also, we can discuss ways to enhance your own sales training with the use of videocassettes!" He looked at me sharply and said, "Go on in and sit down!"

After he was seated behind his desk, he slowly shook his head and said, "You know, you are the first salesman to call on me who actually knew the exact purpose of his call. I appreciate it! Please tell me about your program."

In those few words, this individual dramatically emphasized the purpose of the Curiosity Step. If you have done it correctly, your prospect should say, or think, "Tell me more!"

CHAPTER SUMMARY

Several important revelations in this chapter can make your selling easier and more successful. Please stop a moment to answer this question:

What was the one most important idea you received from this chapter, and how are you going to apply it today?

Some of those revelations were:

- The main reason prospects say, "I'm not interested!" is because the salesperson *was not interesting*.
- You do not arouse interest by asking a question; you are being conversational. You arouse interest by *stating* a big, fat claim bearing upon the prospect's needs, wants, or dominant buying motive.
- The purpose of the Curiosity Step is to get the prospect to want to hear your sales presentation.
- Rise above the ordinary! The Curiosity Step is completely skipped by more salespeople than any other step of the selling process.

- The Curiosity Step gift wraps the presentation and causes the prospect to say, or think, "Tell me more!"
- Bridges are connecting phrases between two different portions, or functions, of the sales interview. They make your sales presentation smoother and more coherent.
- The two bridges one could choose to connect the Conversation Step and the Curiosity Step are:

... the reason I mention this, we have a ... for you, or ... my purpose is ...

- The bridge between the Curiosity Step and the Conviction Step is:

... the name of my product, or program, is ...

CHAPTER 8

The Conviction Step

As THE name of this step implies, it is the one in which we attempt to convince our prospects on the merits of our product, service, or idea so that they can make a favorable, logical decision to buy. Facts, benefits, and evidence are the essential ingredients of this process.

This step is sometimes referred to as the *body* of the sales talk. It is where 99 percent of the salespeople spend almost 99 percent of their time. Although this step is almost always vital for the success of an interview, it is certainly not worthy of this much time.

Since we know people buy from emotion rather than by logic, why do you suppose the Conviction Step is an important part of the sales presentation? It is important because a prospect can rarely become *emotionally* moved to buy until first *logically* convinced it is the right decision to make! A professional salesperson must be capable of determining how much logic is required to accomplish this without burdening the prospect with too much technical information.

In the Conviction Step, four general questions must be answered before a prospect is convinced. They are:

1. What is it?
2. How will it benefit *me*?
3. Is it priced right?
4. Can you prove it?

Since prospects are rarely emotionally moved to buy unless first logically satisfied the decision is right for them, these four questions must be answered to each prospect's satisfaction. Otherwise, later appeals to the emotion will have little or no effect.

The purpose of this chapter is to enable you to be more convincing while, at the same time, becoming more concise. We will learn to distinguish between facts and benefits. We will find another use for bridges in constructing convincing Units of Conviction. Some of these ideas should help you to become more customer oriented and more competitive.

Many salespeople try to be convincing by overwhelming the prospect with facts. They seem to believe the more the prospect knows about the product, the better the chance for the sale. Sometimes a prospect is just not interested in all of those facts.

An unforgettable example of this happened recently when a close friend tried to convince me of the need for a water purifier in my home. I have no doubt about his unbridled enthusiasm and belief in his product. I heard about the dangers of chlorine, salts, pollution, and bacteria until it was nearly nauseating. I began to wonder how I had lived so long! I heard about the inferiority of his competitor in great detail. Certainly, the price was not prohibitive. I found out more about water purifiers than I had ever wanted to know. Believe it or not, his sales presentation lasted for more than an hour with little opportunity for me to talk.

If ever I heard "the whole load," it was in this discussion! I still don't plan to buy a water purifier. The only reason I listened as long as I did was because he is a friend. "A man convinced against his will is of the same opinion still."

Is such a presentation unusual? I am afraid not. I surely can't fault my friend's thoroughness on his preparation of the features. His verbosity only emphasizes a very important observation. *Facts by themselves rarely sell!* Too many facts can have a negative impact unless they are accompanied with personalized customer benefits. These benefits were completely missing in my friend's sales presentation.

To emphasize how facts or features, standing alone, are

unpalatable for the prospect, we conduct an unusual exercise ir our sales training. We ask participants to stand before the class, one at a time, and state a most outstanding feature of their own product. We then ask the class to shout: "SO WHAT!" At first, each salesperson is startled by this. One can learn from this exercise that unless your prospect *assumes* a benefit resulting from a fact you give them, this reaction might be a typical response never voiced! A professional salesperson doesn't take the chance of this assumption.

Facts are like onions—they don't taste very good as a main course. If you were to sit down to dinner and onions were the only thing to eat, it wouldn't look very appetizing, would it? Needed with onions is some "meat." In fact, we prefer having considerably more meat than onions.

The benefits in our presentation can represent the meat of the conviction process. They need to be prepared exactly the way our prospect might prefer them. My friend's presentation had far too many onions, cooked far too long!

Let's start by differentiating between facts and benefits. Study the following comparison.

Facts	Benefits
325 horsepower	Dependable acceleration
Beige in color	Will complement your furniture
10 percent interest	Good return for retirement
Four bedrooms	Be able to have a guest room
Nonstop to New York	No tiring layovers enroute
Battery operated	Can carry it with you

The facts are usually the technical features that distinguish one product from another. The benefits are the individual advantages that are specifically important to each prospect. Please notice that each feature could cause you to think of any number of other benefits.

On a separate sheet of paper write down four of the most important features of your product, service, or idea.

Look again at what you have written and ask yourself whether you have written facts, or are they benefits? It can be confusing, and it is almost always debatable which is which. But, with the use of *bridges*, you don't have to worry! With the use of a few simple bridges within what is called a *Unit of Conviction*, you can be more assured your prospects can appreciate the *benefits* of your product. With the use of bridges, you will always be talking in terms of your prospect's interest in each and every sales presentation. Those bridges, used in a Unit of Conviction are:

because
which means to you
and the real benefit to you is

Remember, the prospect is more easily convinced by benefits that appeal directly to needs, wants, or dominant buying motive (the meat) than by the facts you may present (the onions).

As an example, let me try to convince you of the importance of the *fact* (onion) that bridges are important for you to use. I could just make the following dogmatic statement of this fact by itself:

Bridges will enable you to speak in terms of your prospect's interest!

Please read the sentence again. Are you convinced? Do you readily accept the statement as being important for your consideration? Do you *assume* from this statement that bridges are beneficial to you?

Notice how this feature is supported by a claim and two benefits in a Unit of Conviction.

"You will become much more convincing when using bridges in your sales presentations

because

they will enable you to speak in terms of your prospect's interest.

which means to you

that your prospect will more readily understand the personal advantages of the outstanding features of your product or service,

and the real benefit to you is

the thrill of effortlessly making more sales and profits!"

Read this complete Unit of Conviction aloud. Compare how much more convincing it is than the statement about the feature alone.

A Unit of Conviction is divided into four important components. They are identified as:

> A little, fat claim
> A fact or feature
> A benefit
> A buyer's benefit

In Chapter 7 on the Curiosity Step, we learned that the big, fat claim opens the prospect's mind to the entire sales presentation. In the Unit of Conviction, we have a *little, fat claim*, which opens the prospect's mind to *one* fact or feature.

When does a claim become a fact? . . . only when the *prospect* accepts the claim as a fact. When does a fact become a benefit? . . . only when the *prospect accepts* the fact as a benefit!

Memorize the bridges exactly as worded. Do *not* leave out the two *you*'s. Write a Unit of Conviction around each of the four facts you listed earlier. Then, read them aloud, or practice them on a friend. After you have done this, put away your notes and verbalize a Unit of Conviction around other important features.

LITTLE, FAT CLAIM:

because

FACT:

which means to you

BENEFIT:

and the real benefit to you is

BUYER'S BENEFIT:

WARNING! Do not change a single word of the bridges until you have tried them in interviews at least 25 times.

Based on experience, I can almost hear some of my readers asking: "Isn't the prospect bothered by the repetition of these same phrases?" The truth is the prospect does not hear any redundancy, since what he or she focuses on is . . . *"benefit to you!"* However, with experience, you will discover that you will probably use no more than three or four Units of Conviction in any sales presentation. You use them to emphasize your most salient points.

Take a moment to look back at your buyer's benefit. Chances are it is *emotional* in character. Don't be overly concerned about trying to make it an emotional benefit when first trying to develop Units of Conviction. You will find that with the proper use of the bridges, it will generally happen automatically. As in the Curiosity Step, we have another introduction of the use of emotions in your selling interview. Bridges in the Unit of Conviction can help you appeal to the emotions without conscious effort.

The price of a product is, in sales terminology, a *fact*. It can be a distasteful onion when it stands alone! For some salespeople, it is a traumatic experience to introduce the price of their product to the customer. Some seem almost apologetic in their reluctance to mention it. The prospect gains an advantage whenever the salesperson shows hesitancy and has to be asked for the cost. There is a subtle suggestion the price is high and can be negotiated. Whenever the cost is wrapped in a Unit of Conviction, it can become palatable . . . and undisputed. For example:

"You will consider this vacation the best bargain vacation you have ever had *because* the entire five-day cruise up the Rhine River is only $1,420 per person, *which means to you* the enjoyment of a panorama of sightseeing experiences, such as castles, Dutch windmills, vineyards, and magnificent cathedrals. *The real benefit to you* will be complete, luxurious relaxation as this panoramic view seems to glide by each day of your cruise!"

Doesn't this Unit of Conviction sound better than saying: "The five-day Rhine cruise will cost you and your wife $2,840!"

Perhaps I can shock some price-conscious salespeople by saying, without reservation, people *never* buy any article because of its price. People never buy *any* fact or feature (including price); they buy *what it will do for them*. In this same line of reasoning, IF your prospects can buy *exactly the same thing* for less money, then this is what they should do. To be able to sell our product at a higher

83

price, we must substantiate it with benefits. We must show that it is not "exactly the same."

Now, take a moment to wrap the cost of your own product, or service, into a Unit of Conviction:

LITTLE, FAT CLAIM:

because

FACT: Your investment is only $\$$_____

which means to you

BENEFIT:

and the real benefit to you is

BUYER'S BENEFIT:

NOTE: In an earlier chapter, we spoke of words commonly used in the selling profession, such as *cold calls*, that have a negative connotation. *Cost* is another word. Rather than speaking of *cost* to a prospect, replace it with *investment*, such as is done for you in your Unit of Conviction.

Never again fear to reveal the price of your product. Substantiate it with an individualized Unit of Conviction. Boldly state the benefits that will accrue for your prospect by making the investment. You might rationalize any fears away with yet another perspective. Ask yourself why you should be apprehensive about stating the price—it is the "poor" prospect who has to spend the money!

We are not attempting to handle the objections in this particular chapter, as they will be covered extensively later. What we are setting forth, though, is the obligation of salespeople in the Conviction Step of the sale. Suffice it to say, we should not argue about price; we must *justify it*. Nor can we change the features of the product because of some perceived unfavorable comparison. But, we must look for other advantages despite these disadvantages. If we are incapable of doing this, we should not recommend a buying decision.

The Conviction Step is one in which the presence of a salesperson's confident mental attitude, or CMA, plays a major role! Certainly, one must be enthusiastic to cause the prospect to become enthusiastic (see Chapter 1). A deep belief in the benefits you present to the prospect can help to make the sales talk sparkle! When you use well-prepared Units of Conviction, which appeal to the prospect's needs, wants, or dominant buying motive, your CMA will be apparent.

Jack Degenhard, an agent for Prudential Insurance Company, confirmed the importance of Units of Conviction:

"Before the course, I was suffering with a bad case of call reluctance. However, I continued to make calls, but the results were ghastly. After the training, I asked my manager, Paul Boyer, to help me develop Units of Conviction. On one of my [subsequent] appointments, one man said, "You know, Jack, this is the third time I've had insurance explained to me, but it is the first time I've understood it. That's because no one explained it to me the way you just did. I want you to know I really appreciate it." Thanks to Units of Conviction I now look forward to making calls!"

Sometimes additional evidence is required to support your Units of Conviction before a prospect can be convinced. Although it is possible for facts and benefits to be sufficient, often we may have to provide additional proof. Seven forms of evidence can be used:

> Demonstrations
> Exhibits
> Facts
> Story-type examples
> Analogies
> Testimonials
> Statistics

Demonstrations. If a car salesperson were to tell you his or her new model rides comfortably, you would expect a demonstration ride to prove it. Many products require demonstrations as evidence of their superior performance.

Exhibits. Samples, posters, and literature, plus many other forms of written material about the product, can be very convincing. The display of the product, by itself, can be used as evidence of its merits in some situations.

Facts. Sometimes simply stating facts or features, as we have done in Units of Conviction, is sufficient to prove our statements. Contrary to our statement that facts are like "onions," sometimes facts alone can be effectively used as a form of evidence.

Story-type examples. Relating the experiences of satisfied customers is often used to prove statements made about a product's capabilities. A concise story about the successful usage of a product can be very convincing to a prospect.

Analogies. Perhaps the most powerful kind of evidence is an analogy—the comparison of two *unlikes*. More specifically, a good sales analogy is the comparison of a technical, sophisticated product with an item familiar to the prospect stated in a layperson's terms. For example:

A registered representative in one of my investment classes was having difficulty convincing a widow to sell some of her portfolio bought by her late husband. Visiting her at her home, he found her tending her flower garden.

86

"What do you do, Mrs. Jones, when you have a plant wither as a result of a disease?" he asked.

"Oh, I dig it out and replace it with a new plant," she quickly answered.

"You know, that is much like what needs to be done in your portfolio from time to time," he said. "Sometimes you have to 'dig out' inactive stocks and replace them with new, vibrant ones!"

This powerful analogy was very convincing, and he received a sizable order. Mrs. Jones may not have understood the technical aspects of investing in the market, but she did understand flower gardening!

Testimonials. Written testimonials by satisfied customers can effectively convince some prospects. For conciseness, it may be advisable for *you* to write the essence of your customer's favorable statements about your product, given permission, on his or her letterhead. Doing this allows you to make the testimonial more succinct and more usable. Then, you should highlight the most important sentences. When you use it, your prospect's attention will be quickly focused upon the essential points in the testimonial.

NOTE: Memorize the essential points of your best testimonials and use them as story-type examples. You can then use the written testimonials to back up the story if needed!

Statistics. Although sometimes considered the "driest" of all of the forms of evidence, statistics can be very useful. In some instances, especially in the more technical sales, the use of statistics is vital.

Which of these seven forms of evidence do you use most often? Have you used the same evidence over and over until it seems monotonous even to you? Are you always on the alert for more convincing material that will substantiate your claims? Sometimes it can take months to get just the right story, analogy, or other form of evidence that universally will persuade prospects to understand the superiority of your proposal.

This chapter has dealt primarily with how you can effectively present your product's features and benefits in such a manner that they might appeal individually to each of your prospects. Also, we have discussed how best to use evidence whenever it is necessary to support your statements. In the next four chapters, we will remain in this important Conviction Step, learning how to be more sensitive to your prospect's acceptance, skepticism, or outright rejection of your presentation of ideas. With this sensitivity, you can keep more in command, but not obvious command, of the interview.

CHAPTER SUMMARY

The Conviction Step, sometimes known as the "heart" of the sales presentation, is the logical part of your interview. To prepare yourself for the sophistication of the next few chapters, it might be especially important to answer this question:

What was the one most important idea you received from this chapter, and how are you going to apply it today?

To enable you to be more convincing, the important features of this chapter's summary might be:

- A prospect can rarely become emotionally moved to buy until first logically convinced it is the right decision.
- Before a prospect is convinced, four general questions must be answered to his or her satisfaction:

1. What is it?
2. How will it benefit *me?*
3. Is it priced right?
4. Can you prove it?

- Facts by themselves rarely sell. They often cause the prospect mentally to say: "SO WHAT!"
- Benefits and buyer's benefits are the "meat" of the conviction process.
- A Unit of Conviction consists of four parts:

  —A little, fat claim
  —A fact or feature
  —A benefit
  —A buyer's benefit

- The important bridges in the Unit of Conviction are:

because
which means to you
and the real benefit to you is

- Prospects never buy because of the price of the article . . . they buy because of what it will do for them.
- Price, cost, and investment are facts. Whenever you quote a price, it should *always* be wrapped in a Unit of Conviction.
- A salesperson's enthusiasm should play an important role in the Conviction Step.
- Enhance your power to be convincing with the use of the seven forms of evidence. Can you name them?

CHAPTER 9

Sensitivity in Closing

WHILE DRIVING to a sales call with an Australian distributor near Melbourne, my associate and I happened to be listening to a program about personal communication on an educational radio station. A somewhat startling statement was made that 60 percent of all communication is done by body language, 20 percent by the inflection of the voice, and 20 percent by the spoken word. If this statement is anywhere near correct, it suggests that keen observation and acute listening practices tell us more about what is going on in our prospects' minds than the words they use!

Are you aware of the subliminal communications going on between you and your prospect throughout the sales interview? Do you get a "feeling" when a prospect is ready to buy, and can you accurately identify the feeling? Have you ever wondered whether or not you may have missed a perfect chance to make a sale? Think about it for a moment. Why *do* you sometimes get a feeling when it is the right time to ask for the order? Are there clues that help you to know exactly when to close?

The purposes of this chapter are to provide you with an instrument to uncover your prospect's feelings throughout the interview and to increase your sensitivity to the many signposts you can "read" along the way. Like traffic signs displayed on the highway, these indicators jump out at the alert salesperson. They say, "I'll take it," "I'm not quite convinced," and "I like what I'm hearing." They literally signal caution, stop, or go during the interview. They also can tell you when the order is there for the asking, long before the prospect is aware of it.

First, we will help you avoid a common, and deadly, hazard—talking past the point of the sale. You will learn surefire means to probe for a prospect's feelings at any time in the interview. These probes will accurately tell you where the prospect is in the steps of the sale. Remember, a prospect works through all of the stages before buying, even if you don't cover them all in your presentation.

TALKING PAST THE SALE

An all-too-common problem is that many salespeople "sell a product in 5 minutes, and buy it back in the next 35 by talking too much." This happens more often than you might suspect. An experienced salesperson is far less apt to commit this error than is a newer one. Seasoned salespeople will quickly admit they "just get a feeling when to close" but rarely can they specifically identify exactly *what* they feel. We'll provide that identification in this chapter.

The first sensitivity a salesperson must work to develop is how not to talk past the "point" of the sale. I can teach you how to avoid this common pitfall by using a simple phrase, which introduces questions weighted in varying degrees of intensity. These gentle, probing questions are designed to give you a remarkably reliable indication of prospects' feelings while, at the same time, giving them full credit for their intelligence. Sound too easy to be true, almost magical? We will call them Magic Questions because they work almost like magic.

You can best understand the value of Magic Questions if you could first get into the habit of asking Trial Closes every once in a while after stating important facts. For example:

The interest return on this issue last year was 10.5 percent, nontaxable. *In your opinion, do you feel* that is attractive?

The gas mileage on this model in highway driving is about 35 miles per gallon. *In your opinion, do you feel* this is appealing?

91

Your hotel room overlooks the beautiful blue Pacific, and the sandy beach comes right up to the door! *In your opinion, do you feel* the sounds of the sea would lull you to sleep at night?

The above Trial Closes are nearly equal in weight, and each is comparatively "heavy." However, sprinkled throughout your interview, such questions allow you to judge the buying temperature without prospects feeling they are getting the third degree.

A more subtle, sophisticated probing could be accomplished by the use of Magic Questions. By definition, Magic Questions are "weighted" Trial Closes. They can vary in intensity from "light" to "light heavy" to "heavy" if they are developed from your Units of Conviction.

Let's analyze a sales situation in which you feel the need to determine whether or not your prospect is really accepting your recommendation: You are in the Conviction Step of the sale. You feel you can achieve the greatest effect by giving a Unit of Conviction about one of the most important features of your product. You observe a flicker of interest from your prospect, but can't really judge how well you have communicated. In other words, you need to probe for the true feelings of the prospect before proceeding further into your sales talk.

Starting with the Unit of Conviction:

SALESPERSON: "This hedge trimmer will work best for you

because

it cuts a 24-inch swath,

which means to you

you can reach farther back across your hedge and take less strokes to cut it.

92

and the real benefit to you is

it will be much less tiring to complete your trimming each time."

SALESPERSON (Purpose-Permission): *"My purpose* at this time *is* to get your *answers* to a few questions. Do you mind if I ask them?"

PROSPECT: "No, I don't mind."

SALESPERSON: (Magic Question #1—"light"): *"In your opinion, do you feel* you would like to trim your big hedges easier?"

PROSPECT: "Certainly!"

SALESPERSON (Magic Question #2—"light heavy"): *"In your opinion, do you feel* the size of your hedge warrants a longer hedge trimmer?"

PROSPECT: "Sometimes I have to use a stepladder. It's frustrating."

SALESPERSON (Magic Question #3—"heavy"): "Then, *in your opinion, do you feel* a 24-inch trimmer would save you this aggravation?"

PROSPECT: "I think it could save me an hour each time I have to do this dreaded job!"

SALESPERSON (Order-Asking Question): "Do you want to use your American Express card?"

At first glance, this procedure can seem complicated. Once you understand its construction, and its value, it can be very straightforward and simple. Here is what was done:

1. Unit of Conviction around outstanding feature.
2. Purpose-Permission Technique, which causes more openness in answering your questions. (To be used only *one time* in a sales presentation.)
3. Magic Question rephrasing the buyer's benefit.
4. Magic Question rephrasing the benefit.

5. Magic Question rephrasing the fact.
6. Order-Asking Question if it is apparent a buying decision has been made.

ANALYZING MAGIC QUESTIONS

Repeating . . . Magic Questions are *weighted, probing Trial Closes*, starting first with the rephrasing of the buyer's benefit . . . second, with the rephrasing of the benefit . . . and third, with the rephrasing of the fact. *Weighted* refers to their ease of answering. The easier to answer, the lighter the weight.

Reexamine the weight of each Magic Question in our example. Because the easiest question for the prospect to answer is the one designed around the buyer's benefit, it is called "light." In this particular instance, it would be very easy for the person who dreads the hedge-trimming chore to answer it affirmatively.

Notice the second Magic Question, designed around the benefit, tends to focus the prospect's attention toward the use of the product. Thus, there might be a slight reluctance to agree with the salesperson. This possible resistance causes the question to be labeled "light heavy."

The "heavy" question is centered only on one specific feature of the product. The prospect may subconsciously realize that with the "buying" of this feature *might* come a commitment to the purchase of the entire product. No one likes to make a decision!

Technically speaking, though, this "heavy" Magic Question is *still* relatively easy for the prospect. It is not too heavy because the prospect is rendering an opinion about only *one* of your many product features. This is NOT the case had the question been, *"In your opinion, do you feel* you would like to buy a 24-inch hedge trimmer today?" Such a heavy question puts the entire product up for acceptance or rejection. Whenever such a "very heavy" question is used, the salesperson is left with little ammunition should the prospect say, "No!"

If you receive an enthusiastic answer to ANY of these Magic Questions, it is a strong indication a buying decision has been made. As with any Trial Close, however, the answer could be a "yes," "no," or "maybe."

A great advantage of using Magic Questions for probing is that it keeps the salesperson from putting the entire proposition on the selling block. In this example, if the prospect rejects the 24-inch feature, dozens of features are still left to present.

It is human nature for a prospect to refrain from answering when he or she either consciously or subconsciously senses a decision is close at hand. Therefore, the subtle, gradual effect of these Magic Questions probes for a response without causing the prospect any discomfort. As you probe, you get an indication of the prospect's buying "temperature" at any given moment in the interview. Therefore, you remain in command, but not obvious command, of your sales presentation.

Now, it is time for you to practice the development of Magic Questions from a Unit of Conviction. Think of one of the most important features you intend to present in your next interview. Incidentally, the Purpose-Permission Technique included in your format is another very successful, gracious way to cause your prospect to *want* to give you answers to any number of questions.

LITTLE, FAT CLAIM:

because

FACT:

which means to you

BENEFIT:

and the real benefit to you is

BUYER'S BENEFIT:

"My purpose at this time is to get your answers to a few questions. Do you mind if I ask them?"

light magic question around buyer's benefit:
light heavy magic question around benefit:
heavy magic question around fact:
minor decision-asking question:

Please read the entire procedure aloud for practice. In your first few practices, assume all "yes" answers from the prospect. Practice this with an associate before you use it in the field, repeating the *purposes* of the Magic Questions: They help you to understand whether or not your prospect accepts, or buys, your important feature; sometimes the response tells you the prospect has bought your entire proposal! The answers to the Magic Questions can also indicate if you are "on the right track" in your presentation.

COMMUNICATIONS YOU CAN'T HEAR

Modern research has provided many insights into interpersonal communication. Assuming 60 percent of all communication is done by body language and 20 percent by vocal inflection, this means that only 20 percent of our communications counts on the spoken word.

This formula applies especially well in the process of closing a sale! As stated before, ask any experienced salespeople how they know when to close, and many will answer they "get a feeling." Ask what that feeling is . . . and few can put their finger on it. What they have trouble pinpointing are *buying signals*.

You can learn to identify specific buying signals and greatly enhance your ability to close the sale. You can also learn to recognize indicators of negative feelings, which enable

you to sense the need for a different direction in your interview.

Recognizing buying signals has helped thousands of salespeople
to cut their selling time in half, which means to you that closing
will be more fun and easier. *The real benefit is* that you can lead
your company in sales. *In your opinion, do you feel* you would like
to be #1? . . . *In your opinion, do you feel* that you would like to have
more fun while closing? . . . *In your opinion, do you feel* it would be
worth your time to concentrate on identifying buying signals?

Let's start with the terminology.

BUYING SIGNALS

A buying signal is anything a prospect *says* or *does* that indicates he
or she has reached a favorable decision and has *already bought!*

A buying signal is an indication of *mental ownership* of the
product or service.

NOTE: Perhaps I should accurately specify what I mean by *buy*
before you start to concentrate on this issue. Buying signals usually indicate the prospect has bought your entire proposal or
product. However, these signals *might* mean the prospect has
bought only one or two of your product's features. You may need
to probe to find out exactly what has taken place.

VOCAL BUYING SIGNALS

First, let us consider what a prospect might *say* that would be a
buying signal.

"I'll take it."

If you should hear your prospect say this, I assume you'd assume! The only thing wrong with getting this response is you have

probably *missed* at least ten other buying signals prior to the time a prospect says it.

Now, make your own judgment. Which of the following are buying signals? Remember, if you hear a buying signal, you should immediately, and unhesitatingly, ask for the order! Put a check beside each one you are *sure* is a buying signal.

"Does this come in yellow?"

"How soon could I expect delivery?"

"What did you say was the horsepower?"

"Does this come with a guarantee?"

"How does the trade-in value compare on this model?"

"What is the price on this?"

If you checked any of the above, you could be right, or you could be dead wrong! Sound confusing? Let's take the guesswork out of it.

The *key question* to ask yourself when in doubt about a buying signal is: "By what the prospect says or does, *does he or she mentally own it*?" If the client does, you have a buying signal! As you listen to the inflection of the voice, listen for ownership. Should you hear questions such as those previously listed, concentrate on the prospect's voice inflection to determine whether he or she is simply asking for information or indicating mental ownership.

However, if you are uncertain about a possible buying signal, you have *already learned* about an instrument to take the prospect's temperature: *"In your opinion, do you feel . . ."*

PROSPECT: "Do they come in yellow?"

SALESPERSON: "They surely do. *In your opinion, do you feel* you prefer that color?"

PROSPECT: "Yes, I certainly do."
(And now you have a buying signal!)

PROSPECT: "What *is* the price on this?"
SALESPERSON: "It is only $58.95! *In your opinion, do you feel* this is within your budget?"
PROSPECT: "It is a little higher than I intended to pay, but despite this, I like the style."
(Buying signal!)

Remember! Anytime you sense mental ownership, you may have a buying signal. If you are not sure, simply use a Trial Close, or better yet, Magic Questions, to be certain. Sometimes the most innocuous statements by prospects reflect a subconscious decision to buy. Conscientious listening to your prospects' responses can produce unexpected sales results. If you are like most salespeople studying buying signals for the first time, you will be astounded how many you have missed in previous interviews.

How many vocal buying signals are there? . . . literally hundreds. Remember, the key is: "By what they *say* or *do*, do they *mentally* own it?"

Physical Buying Signals

And now, for what prospects *do* that are buying signals. As surprising as some of these might seem to you, these signals have been affirmed by tens of thousands of salespeople. Assuming 60 percent of all communication is by body language, let's identify some of the signs. Let's examine *seven* tried and proven physical buying signals that indicate ownership of a product, service, or idea. These are nearly infallible, and should you question their authenticity, simply test them with your buying thermometer.

Sudden relaxation
Sparkling eye
Open hand
Touching the order pad
Touching the chin
Increasing friendliness
Reexamination of the product

Sudden relaxation. Should your prospect suddenly lean forward toward you or back in the chair, from a position of tension, you may have a buying signal. Sometimes you may see or hear a deep, unexpected sigh during your presentation. Be careful! *Any* sudden relaxation should cause you to ask yourself if a buying signal is present. If you are not absolutely certain, simply test with, *"In your opinion, do you feel . . ."*

Sparkling eye. You have certainly seen the sparkling eye when around happy children. Did you know that if in the "heat" of an interview, your prospect's eyes sparkle, it is time to close?

I vividly remember a sales presentation at Don Drennan Chevrolet in Birmingham, Alabama. I was in front of about 15 prospects and had just finished my Conversation Step and Curiosity Step when I noticed one man's eyes sparkle. I quickly looked around at the rest of my audience and saw no other sparkling eyes. I couldn't believe I could have a buying signal within the first 5 minutes of my presentation! I had been introduced to everyone before the meeting and remembered this man's name, Mel Lively. So, I stopped what I had intended to say and asked a Magic Question:

"Mel, in your opinion, do you feel you could attend a weekly Thursday evening session in our sales training program?"

He looked somewhat startled but said, "Sure!" I immediately gave him an enrollment card. He glanced around at his associates and then signed up.

After the meeting, he asked me why I had picked on him so early. I answered, with a chuckle, that he would find out in Session 6 about the buying signal he had given me.

The important lesson to be learned from this example is that a buying signal occurred even before I presented the features and benefits of my product. Mel was hardly more startled than I.

Is it possible you may have missed this particular buying signal in the past?

Open hand. People often communicate very expressively with their hands. Notice your prospects' hands while they are talking. A clenched fist can mean determination or anger; a pointing finger can be accusatory; and an open hand can be a *buying signal!*

If you should notice your prospect's hand(s) resting on the table or desk in front of him or her in an open, palms-up position, it may be time to ask for the order, especially if you should see this signal as a sudden change from a clenched fist or a wringing of hands. It is certainly worth an immediate Trial Close to find out what the prospect is feeling.

Touching the order pad. Often, I've been asked when one should get the order form out in front of the prospect. The answer is simple—*early*. Keep it in plain view during the presentation. Don't whip it out late in the interview like a pistol! *Why?* One important reason is that the presence of the order pad may give you an opportunity to observe a surprising buying signal.

If the order pad, or contract, is lying out in the open, you may see the prospect suddenly touch it or even pick it up. If so, the selling process is usually over! If you find this hard to believe, and see it happen, test the prospect with a couple of Magic Questions. This applies also to literature you may have brought along with you. Should prospects pick up any such article, stop selling! Wait

101

for them to finish their reading, and then ask, *"In your opinion, do you feel . . ."*

Far too many salespeople disregard this movement and talk right past a key point in the sale. As I've said, "Salespeople talk themselves out of more sales than they talk themselves into!"

Touching the chin. I don't know of anything that works 100 percent of the time in selling . . . except this buying signal! If, during the interview, you see your prospect suddenly touch his or her chin in any manner, *you have a positive, reliable buying signal.*

Probably no other feature of my sales training program causes more comment . . . nor raises more initial skepticism . . . than this buying signal. It seems inconceivable, at first, that such a gesture can be so infallible. If you haven't been aware of this signal before, it can be both surprising and humorous.

Conversely, a *negative* signal that is almost as accurate as the touching of the chin is the touching of the nose! When a prospect touches the nose, it means, "I don't agree . . . I don't believe . . . I don't buy that!" Should you use a Trial Close at this precise moment, the prospect will verbalize negative feelings.

In 30 years I've had but one student tell me the touching-the-chin gesture wasn't always accurate. I remember my surprise when one salesperson in Augusta, Georgia, reported back to the class that the "chin" buying signal didn't work. When I asked him to describe the interview, he said:

> "I was trying to sell insurance to a man who had his hand on his chin practically the entire evening. At least a dozen times I asked for the order, but I didn't get it."

Frankly, I was very puzzled, and remarked I must be in error by saying it is 100 percent accurate. Then, I happened to ask him to show the class how this individual was holding his chin. He put his hand over his mouth holding *both* the nose and the chin! I broke out laughing because I realized I had forgotten to tell this

102

class about the negative nose signal. Rather than receiving a positive buying signal, he was actually receiving a very strong negative one.

In another class, a salesperson reported seeing a negative nose signal early in the interview, and then the prospect's fingers moved down to the lips!

"I didn't know what to do, so I just kept right on selling. The prospect's hand went on down to the chin. I asked for the order, and was out of the house with it in less than eight minutes!"

The fingers on the lips denotes *indecision*. The salesperson was absolutely correct in continuing to sell.

You don't trust this buying signal yet? Whenever you see it, prove it to yourself by stopping whatever you are discussing in the interview and use a Trial Close. Only, please, don't do what some salespeople have done by laughing out loud the first few times the touching of the chin is found to be accurate!

Increasing friendliness. Have you ever had a prospect suddenly *interrupt* you during an interview to offer a refreshment or a courtesy? "Would you like a cup of coffee?" "Let's go in the den where we'll be more comfortable."

With the offer of coffee, most salespeople reply, "Yes, a coffee is fine." They then let the prospect go to brew the coffee . . . *and lose the sale!*

An interruption of any kind that shows a sudden increase of friendliness can be a strong buying signal. If you are not certain, use a Trial Close before you accept the courtesy, such as, "Yes! I would enjoy a coffee, but before you get it, *in your opinion, do you feel* a Monday delivery is soon enough?" Get the order first, and then *enjoy the coffee*. It tastes so much better!

Reexamination of the product. Beware of the situation in which a prospect suddenly reviews a feature, a piece of literature, or the product itself! It may be a buying signal in disguise. If you keep on talking, you may talk past the point of the sale.

For example, in selling real estate, a prospect, having been shown through a home, might suddenly ask to walk back into the house for a minute. The salesperson should follow to see if the prospect shows mental ownership of some feature of the home. The prospect may want to measure a wall, cabinet, or room, indicating a mental placement of some piece of furniture or appliance. This physical manifestation of mental ownership is a definite buying signal.

In describing vocal and physical buying signals, the word *suddenly* is used repeatedly. Almost all buying signals do happen suddenly. So suddenly, in fact, it will startle you, and you will be tempted not to believe the order is there for your asking!

Buying signals are subconscious acts. Certainly, the prospect is totally unaware of them. If you are truly observant, and a very conscientious listener, you should be able measurably to reduce your selling time.

In fact, it is possible to close too quickly and a little selling "after the fact" may be necessary. Should you observe your prospect having second thoughts after the sale is made, it may be necessary for you to review a few key benefits before leaving. A Unit of Conviction plus Magic Questions might be very appropriate if you sense the prospect is uneasy. Don't worry: If your buying signals were accurate, you won't miss the sale. You are just reassuring the prospect of a wise decision.

You should now have the answer to the "feeling" you have had when it is time to close. It is hoped, learning about buying signals will heighten your awareness to these feelings and help you act on these indications far more quickly than you have in the past.

When do you ask for the order? As stated previously several times, you ask for the order when the prospect has *already bought*. Recognizing buying signals is the means of knowing exactly when it has taken place!

CHAPTER SUMMARY

This chapter is often the most exciting one for those experienced salespeople who have sensed buying signals but have never had them identified. Compare your own feelings about this chapter by asking yourself this question:

What was the one most important idea you received from this chapter, and how are you going to apply it today?

Some of the more important ideas presented include:

- Sixty percent of all communication is done by body language, 20 percent by the inflection of the voice, and only 20 percent by the spoken word.

- Some salespeople sell a product in 5 minutes and buy it back in the next 35, by talking too much.

- Magic Questions are *weighted* Trial Closes; starting with "light" (about the buyer's benefit), "light heavy" (about the benefit), and "heavy" (about the fact or feature).

- The Purpose-Permission Technique puts you in command, but not obvious command, of the interview. It should be used only one time during a presentation.

- A buying signal is anything a prospect says or does that indicates he or she has reached a favorable decision and has already bought.

- The two types of buying signals are vocal and physical.

- If you are unsure whether or not you have sensed a buying signal, *immediately* use a Trial Close to check it out.

- Can you identify the *seven* physical buying signals?

- *All* buying signals happen *suddenly*. A professional salesperson remains acutely observant while listening and watching for them.
- You must be able to forget about yourself to remain alert enough to sense buying signals.

CHAPTER 10

Facing Up to Objections

WHAT IS your personal reaction to objections? Do you dread and fear them? Do you think you need to have a profound answer that will somehow "overcome" each objection in order to be successful? Or, do you have a sense of inadequacy when objections arise that causes you to shrink from them?

The major purposes of this chapter are twofold: (1) to help cause you to relax when you receive objections, and (2) to learn to probe any adverse reaction from your prospect in order to determine whether or not such an objection is real. Please don't be in a hurry to find "answers" to your prospects' objections. We will cover this in its entirety in Chapter 12.

One of three different responses can be expected from the prospect after you use a Trial Close, or Magic Question. It will be:

yes
maybe
no!

Until now, we have concentrated on selling situations in which the prospect was positively inclined toward buying. We have intentionally disregarded objections, which, by their very nature, interrupt the sales interview, in order to concentrate on the selling principles you were learning. It is time to consider those cases in which the prospect says a "maybe" or "no!"

The major purpose of the next *three* chapters is to enable you to handle, classify, and answer objections without antagonizing the

107

prospect. The real benefit to you will be an attitude of complete confidence to handle all objections. *In your opinion, do you feel* these chapters might ease your mind and make selling more fun?

We will start with two important and somewhat startling premises:

1. More sales are lost because salespeople attempt to answer objections that *are not real* than for any other reason!
2. The problem most salespeople have with objections is *not the problem of knowing* how *to answer them,* but in how to *find* the real, blocking objection(s) to answer!

If your sales talk is well prepared and succinctly attuned to your client's interests, objections are not too likely to occur. You probably won't receive *any* objections in one out of five interviews. Although 20 percent of the time the sale is made without encountering objections, four out of five times a professional should *expect* to receive objections in an interview.

Many salespeople not only fear objections but seem demoralized and intimidated by them. Some quickly lose their enthusiasm and conviction once objections are raised and they feel defeated. If objections normally arise 80 percent of the time, a salesperson should be surprised if none occurs!

The first premise of this chapter states, "More sales are lost because salespeople attempt to answer objections that are not real than for any other reason." Does it make any sense to answer objections that the prospect does not really mean? How is it possible such a common fault exists among salespeople? Are you guilty of attempting to answer objections that are not real? "Surely not!" you must be thinking.

Why do prospects play games with you by disguising their real feelings and give you phantom objections they don't really mean? Why do prospects deliberately try to hide their real objections? The cause of this subterfuge is their subconscious fear of having to make a decision should their real blocking objection become known by you. They sense a decision to buy might be imminent should you hear the real objection and answer it.

Does this sound illogical to you? Let's put you to the test! Look at the following statements and ask yourself if you have ever raised similar objections when someone was trying to sell to YOU:

"I'm just looking."
"I can't afford to pay that much."
"I need to think about it."
"I'll have to shop around a bit more."
"Your price is out of line."
"I need to talk it over with my wife (husband)."

If you used these statements, were they honest ones? Or did you say them to avoid disclosing your real resistance to buying, and hence, try to stall any further discussion of the product? Such objections are often meant to slow down, or stop, the selling process, and rarely reflect the real feelings of the prospect. Accepting such trite comments without question may cause a salesperson to lose the sale unnecessarily. Certainly, we owe it to ourselves, and to our prospects, to determine exactly what is behind such statements.

Are you aware there are rarely more than two or three real, hereinafter called *blocking*, objections in the average interview? By blocking objection, I'm referring to those that can actually block the prospect from making a favorable commitment. In fact, should you receive more than three objections in any interview, you can "bet your bottom dollar" the prospect is *hiding* the blocking one.

Before learning how to handle objections, let's briefly identify the proper attitude toward them. The right attitude to have . . . is to *love* objections! A professional knows it is usually impossible to find out what is really on the prospect's mind until objections are out in the open. Loving objections may be expecting a lot, but if you don't appreciate the important role that objections play in uncovering your prospect's feelings and if you can't enjoy the verbal sparring involved in handling and answering objections, sales interviews will always be painful.

Some salespeople seem so startled when an objection appears, we refer to the rejection as an "explosive NO!" Handling and finding the blocking objection is the key to determining its importance to the prospect, and whether or not it has the potential of derailing the sale. Let's look at the most common, but *wrong*, way to handle it before we uncover a much more successful technique.

There is a one-word response that salespeople use almost every time they encounter "the explosive NO!" That word is *why?* The "Why?" response speaks *down* to the prospect. It is demeaning, challenging, and sometimes insulting.

Look at these examples. Notice the possible implication of the "Why?" shown in parentheses.

PROSPECT: "No!"
SALESPERSON: "Why?"

PROSPECT: "I can't afford it."
SALESPERSON: "Why?"
(You look successful enough . . . or can't you recognize a bargain when you see one?)

PROSPECT: "No!"
SALESPERSON: "Why?"
PROSPECT: "Your price is too high!"
SALESPERSON: "Why do you say that?"
(Can't you see the quality you're getting? You've been paying for junk in the past.)

The implications of "Why?" and the tone of voice of the salesperson not only challenge the beliefs of prospects but also fail to give any credit for intelligence. No matter what inflection in the voice is used to deliver this "Why?" it is virtually impossible to eliminate the condescending impression it leaves. If you have been using "Why?" regularly, it will take a great deal of concentration to eliminate this bad habit.

Now that we've removed the "Why?" from your repertoire, let's replace it with a truly effective tool for dealing with objections. The two-step process is called the Obviously You—Jes Supposin' Technique and is designed to:

1. Stop the prospect from sidetracking the motion, or direction, of the sale.
2. Test the validity of the objection by attempting to bury it.
3. Bury phantom, or invalid, objections without embarrassing the prospect.
4. Isolate those objections that might be real and need answering.

The two step technique is:

1. *"Obviously you have some reason for saying that. Do you mind if I ask what it is?"*

Listen carefully to the answer, and . . .

2. *"Just supposing, for the moment, this was not a concern. Then, in your opinion, do you feel . . ."*

Study the words carefully. Read them out loud a few times and memorize them. Use the *exact* wording of this technique. Experience tells us if you change anything you may not get the desired results. Should you say, for example, "Obviously, you have a reason for saying that. What is it?" This change makes it about as bad as "Why?"

111

Let's analyze each of the parts of this technique separately.

Obviously you. The purpose of this portion of the technique is to soften the effects of the objection and respectfully probe for the real blocking objection. For example:

PROSPECT: "I can't afford it."
SALESPERSON: "Obviously, you have some reason for saying that. Do you mind if I ask what it is?"
PROSPECT: "No, I don't mind."
SALESPERSON: "What is it?"
PROSPECT: "I need to compare prices!"

With the proper vocal inflections, in effect, you are saying, "Look! You are a very intelligent person. I've never heard this kind of response before. I'd like to learn from you . . . do you mind if I ask about it?" How much more courteous and respectful this is than an abrupt "Why?" and *look what you have uncovered*: "I can't afford it" and "I need to compare prices!" are two completely different answers! Do you suppose either are real and blocking?

Another example:

PROSPECT: "Your price is too high!"
SALESPERSON: "Obviously, you have some reason for saying that. Do you mind if I ask what it is?"
PROSPECT: "No, I don't mind."
SALESPERSON: "Then, what is it, please?"
PROSPECT: "I really have other priorities in my budget."

Again, you have two completely different objections! Which one are you supposed to believe? Which objection do you suppose is blocking? This normal disparity in response is the major reason you need to test the objection. The testing is done by attempting to "bury" it with the Jes Supposin' Technique:

Jes Supposin'—The colloquialism Jes Supposin' reminds you to check the response you get from your Obviously You question. The purpose of this portion of the technique is to test its validity by *attempting* to bury the objection received. If you can bury it, the objection is invalid. If the prospect reiterates the objection and sticks by it, this may be the objection that needs to be answered.

Look at several more examples:

SALESPERSON: . . . after receiving permission from Obviously You
    ". . . What is it, please?"
PROSPECT: "I never make up my mind the first night!"
SALESPERSON: "Just supposing, for the moment, this was not a concern. Then, in your opinion, do you feel this policy would give you an added sense of security?"

PROSPECT: "It seems to be a sizable investment."
SALESPERSON: "Just supposing, for the moment, the size of the investment was not a concern. *In your opinion, do you feel* an added sense of security is extremely important to you?"
PROSPECT: "Sure, if the cost wasn't so high, but it is!"

Note how the dogmatic statement " . . . make up my mind the first night" was buried. However, the prospect didn't allow this to happen to "the size of the investment!" It should be apparent to you that the salesperson may have to justify the cost to convince the prospect.

With practice, you will learn to rephrase the prospect's reason in this technique. This rephrasing can then replace "this was not a concern" in the technique. When you do this, you must meet the prospect's condition *exactly!* For example:

PROSPECT: "I can't afford it!"
SALESPERSON: "Just suppose, for the moment, you *could* afford it.

Then, *in your opinion, do you feel* the safety features of this product are important to you?"

PROSPECT: "Yes, if I could afford it, but I can't!"

Notice again, this prospect *verified* the objection by repeating it and not allowing it to be buried. It might be assumed the blocking objection to be answered is now uncovered. In Chapter 12, you will learn exactly how to do this.

In many instances, after you have said, "Obviously you . . ." the prospect will give you one of two responses. They are:

"No, I don't mind if you ask."

"I guess I really don't have a good reason!"

Should the prospect say, "No, I don't mind if you ask," you must follow with, *"What is it?"* Listen carefully to the response. You may sense the objection is important and blocking, or you may feel that it isn't. In either case, you should test with Jes Supposin' to confirm your feelings.

From experience in every class, I can almost hear you say, "What if they say, 'Yes, I *do* mind if you ask what it is!'" My first answer is that I've never heard of it happening. If it should ever happen, however, I would unhesitatingly ask, "Obviously you have some reason for saying *that*. Do you mind if I ask what *it* is?" This person chose not to confide in me for some reason, and I would have to find out what it was before proceeding any further in my sales presentation.

Should the prospect say, "I guess I don't have a good reason!" the prospect suddenly realizes the objection is not valid and you never need to answer it.

Perhaps the easiest way to understand this procedure of handling objections is to look at the stair-step diagram in Figure 1. Follow this important analyzation very carefully.

FIGURE 1

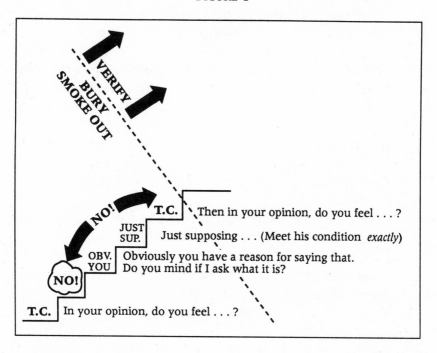

In this example:

Step 1 is a Trial Close.

Step 2 is the prospect's "explosive NO!" (in whatever form the objection might be.)

Step 3 is the Obviously You . . . portion of the technique.

Step 4 is the attempt to bury the objection with Jes Supposin'.

Step 5 is the repetition of the very same Trial Close used in Step 1!

After Step 5, one of three conditions will exist:

1. The objection is *verified,* and you move up the stair steps (in later chapters).*Verified* means the prospect *sticks* to the

objection, and it may be the blocking one you are probing to find. Later on, you may have to answer it.

2. Or, you may *bury* the objection.
3. Or, you may bury the first objection, and *smoke out* an entirely different one. You may then need to test the smoked-out objection, too, with another Obviously You—Jes Supposin' . . . until a blocking objection is verified.

You should *not* go past the dotted line in the diagram until the prospect *sticks to an objection,* and it is therefore *verified.*

Follow the stair-step diagram in the following example:

SALESPERSON: "In your opinion, do you feel the cost-saving feature is important?"

PROSPECT: "NO!"

SALESPERSON: "Obviously, you have some reason for saying that. Do you mind if I ask what it is?"

PROSPECT: "No, I don't mind if you ask."

SALESPERSON: "What is it?"

PROSPECT: "I simply can't afford it."

SALESPERSON: "Just supposing, for the moment, you could afford it. Then, *in your opinion, do you feel* cost saving is important?"

PROSPECT: "NO!"

SALESPERSON: "Obviously, you have some *other* reason for saying that. Do you mind if I ask what it is?"

PROSPECT: "Well, to tell you the truth, I was considering your competitor's model, and I'm not sure if all of the features of your product are better!"

SALESPERSON: "I see! Just suppose, for the moment, our features were superior. Then, *in your opinion, do you feel* the cost-saving feature is our most important benefit to you?"

PROSPECT: "Yes, cost saving is most important. Let's review a comparison of your product with your competitor's."

Look again at our example. Notice the question about "cost saving" was not addressed until the very last! Also, recognize the familiar statement "I can't afford it!" disappeared from the dialogue. In real-life situations, this happens a lot more often than you think!

The Trial Close needs repeating, sometimes again and again, until the prospect answers your question. A courteous repetition of your question *demands* an answer without your being in obvious command of the situation.

I once trained Capt. Jim Haas of the U.S. Army to teach my program in ROTC on college campuses. A couple of years later he reported that this technique did *not* always work, and I asked him to explain.

Well, I met this beautiful girl on base, and I wanted to impress her. So, I took her to a fine restaurant in nearby Williamsburg. When driving her home, I asked, *"In your opinion, do you feel* we should stop off at my apartment for an after-dinner drink?"

"NO!" she said sharply.

"Obviously, you have some reason for saying that," I remarked. "Do you mind if I ask what it is?"

"Look!" she replied. "Turn into this driveway. This is my apartment . . . AND I'VE TAKEN THAT COURSE!"

Poor Jim was shocked, and, for the moment, the technique really hadn't worked. But, I discovered a year later they were married. I'm not exactly sure who sold whom!

In summary, let's review the Obviously You–Jes Supposin' Technique. Three important outcomes result with proper use:

1. The Obviously You Technique avoids conflict and diplomatically probes for the blocking objection.

2. The Jes Supposin' Technique attempts to bury the objection and tests whether or not the objection is important.

3. If the prospect stands by the objection, it *may* need answering if it truly is a blocking objection.

In later chapters, you will learn additional ways to diminish the impact of blocking objections. You will become more aware of the importance of avoiding any kind of confrontation with your prospects.

It is impossible to *overcome* an objection. *Overcome* means fight! We all know the maxim: "Win an argument, lose the sale!" Trying to overcome a prospect's objections is like trying to change a person's religious convictions. And, challenging a prospect's belief's will get you nowhere.

Professional salespeople don't overcome objections; they *handle them and then answer them*. The *handling* process includes relaxing the prospect (and sometimes the salesperson), verifying the authenticity of the objection, and diminishing its impact upon the prospect. *Answering* means empathetically understanding the isolated blocking objection(s), and providing features and benefits designed to substantiate a wise buying decision despite the presence of the objection(s).

CHAPTER SUMMARY

Do objections present more of an exciting challenge to you now? Before proceeding further into handling, analyzing, classifying, and answering objections, it can be important for you to review what you have learned.

Please take a moment to answer our closing question:

What was the one most important idea you received from this chapter, and how are you going to apply it today?

Some major revelations in this chapter are:

• More sales are lost by salespeople because they attempt to answer objections that are not real or do not exist than for any other reason.

• The problem most salespeople have with objections is not in knowing *how* to answer them but in knowing how to *find* the real, blocking objection to answer.

• If you receive more than three objections in an interview, you can be pretty sure the prospect is hiding the blocking one.

• Never use "Why?" when attempting to handle an objection. It is demeaning and speaks down to the prospect.

• Can you list the *four* purposes of the Obviously You–Jes Supposin' Technique?

• The Obviously You–Jes Supposin' Technique gives the prospect credit for his or her intelligence, and helps you avoid challenging the prospect's belief.

• The Obviously You–Jes Supposin' Technique either verifies, buries, or smokes out the objection. This procedure is *not* designed to *answer* it.

• The Obviously You–Jes Supposin' Technique is designed to enable you courteously to smoke out any hidden, blocking objection you may need to answer.

CHAPTER 11

Treat Objections as Questions

A PROFESSIONAL salesperson develops the ability to handle objections with finesse! This means when an opposing viewpoint is raised, the issue is neutralized or answered in such a manner the prospect's beliefs are not openly challenged, and complete respect for the prospect's intelligence is maintained.

How, then, can one effectively get a point across that might be in opposition to a prospect's viewpoint? Even a neophyte in our profession instinctively senses the need to avoid confrontation.

This chapter has two purposes:

1. To reduce chances of argument with the use of Empathy Cushions.
2. To learn to treat *all* blocking objections as nonconfrontational questions that require answering.

EMPATHY CUSHIONS

As the term is meant to imply, a *cushion* is a transitional phrase to "soften" your reply by allowing you to find some area of agreement with the prospect ... before introducing your own opposing views. If you recall, *empathy* is the ability to put yourself in the other person's shoes *without* becoming emotionally involved. Once you believe you have verified the blocking objection, cushions should be used to get some kind of comfortable dialogue started to enable you to keep from hitting the prospect head-on.

Consider the prospect's attitude immediately following the Obviously You–Jes Supposin' Technique. If the objection is verified, inherent in the verification procedure is the prospect saying, "Yes, if it *wasn't* a concern, but *it is!*" A slight irritation in the tone of voice is quite natural as the prospect starts to defend the objection. At this precise moment in the stair-step procedure in handling objections, the prospect's annoyance should be removed. This can be done with cushions.

Let's look at some Empathy Cushions. They are called the *I*, *He/She*, and *They* Cushions and they can be used individually or together. When used concurrently, they become "softer." For example:

I CUSHION: "I understand how you feel..."
HE/SHE CUSHION: "Your friend Joan said exactly the same thing at first..."
THEY CUSHION: "Many people say that at first..."

Notice the softening effect of all three cushions when used together: "I understand how you feel. In fact, your friend Joan said exactly the same thing until investigating further. Most people have the same initial reaction."

CAUTION: Don't use "*I* understand how you feel..." if you *don't* truly understand. If you can't honestly say you understand, then you might quote someone else (the *He/She* Cushion) and/or, if it is applicable, acknowledge that many others have said the same thing (the *They* Cushion). Either, or both, can be effectively used to help you to get in step with your prospect. Any cushion should be used truthfully, with feeling, and with heartfelt empathy.

Frequently, salespeople cause unnecessary arguments by using a seemingly benign phrase. It seems this phrase is an attempt to be agreeable with the prospect, although it actually is *very* confrontational. The phrase is, *"Yes, but! . . ."*

How can one logically say, "Yes, you're right, but you are wrong?" It simply doesn't make sense. Even worse could be the implied message, "Yes, you may be right, . . . *but* you are stupid!" To understand the downside effects of this phrase, consider it in a different context. Suppose one should say, "Yes, your wife is a lady, but! . . ."

Some have said, "Yes, however . . ." is better. Does it sound any less argumentative to say, "Yes, your wife is a lady, however . . ."?

"Yes, but . . ." or "yes, however . . ." should *never* be used on a prospect. In years of working with salespeople, I have found that this is one of the most difficult bad habits to break! The *I, He/She,* and *They* Empathy Cushions are excellent alternatives, yet you may have to work with them for some time before you successfully accomplish your objective of eliminating, "Yes, but! . . ."

Until you break the habit, the "Yes . . . (pause) . . ." phrase might help you. If you catch yourself saying a "yes" when you really didn't mean to say it, try, "Yes . . . (pause) . . . on the other hand have you considered? . . ."

THE TREATED QUESTION

After the Empathy Cushions, the next step in the stair-step process in handling objections is the Treated-Question Technique.

There are two extremely important reasons why it is the professional salesperson's advantage to treat the prospect's blocking objections as questions in disguise:

1. Whenever prospects have objections, they expect to have to defend them and open confrontation might result.
2. If, however, the prospect should find these objections to be questions, the salesperson might have a much better opportunity to answer them!

Before learning the technique, it is very important to analyze what may be going on in the prospect's mind once you have identified (verified) the blocking objection. Let's assume you have used the Obviously You–Jes Supposin' Technique effectively. All indications lead you to believe you know what is blocking your prospect from buying. Let's also assume you have used some Empathy Cushions to soften the prospect's stance. Although the cushions may have reduced the prospect's argumentativeness, an unacceptable adversarial relationship still exists. The prospect knows you are fully aware of the objection and *therefore expects to have to defend it!* The next step must be to eliminate this defensive attitude and disarm the prospect!

THE TREATED-QUESTION TECHNIQUE

"That brings up a question. The question is, would you benefit despite this concern? Is that the question?"

Read and study the examples carefully:

OBJECTION: "Your price is out of line!"
TREATED QUESTION: "That brings up a question. The question is would you benefit despite this concern? Is that the question?"
PROSPECT'S RESPONSE: "Yes. That is the question!"

Should the prospect reply in this manner, rather than an argument ensuing, an opportunity now exists for you to relate additional benefits to help justify your price.

Please note the implied response. It is as though the prospect is now asking, "Can you show me how I would benefit enough to pay that amount of money?" This is *exactly* the frame of mind you want the prospect to have!

The technique, as worded above, is generic and can work in *every* situation. However, customizing the Treated-Question Technique for your specific situation can work even better. The following situation treats the same objection but in a more direct way. This alternative allows you to insert your own words in the Treated Question.

"That brings up a question. The question is? . . . Is that the question?"

OBJECTION: "Your price is out of line!"
TREATED QUESTION: "That brings up a question. The question is, would you benefit enough despite this price to make this investment? Is that the question?"
RESPONSE: "Yes. That is the question exactly!"

Rephrase the prospect's objection indicated by the ellipses, while using *all* of the words in italics *without* change. Be absolutely certain each time you use this technique that you ask, *"Is that the question?"* You *must be certain* the prospect accepts the objection as a question, rather than as an objection!

Practice this technique on your own. Use either the generic or alternate Treated Question form. The objection is:

"I don't have the time to get involved right now. That brings up a question. The question is . . . Is that the question?"

After you have filled in the lines, read it aloud, or better yet, practice it with an associate. Your alternate form should be something like . . . "The question is, *would you benefit enough* to get involved at this time. Is that the question?"

There are three different responses that you might expect while using this technique. When you ask, "Is that the question?" you may hear:

1. "Yes. That is the question." You are now free to answer this particular question stating benefits that justify your position.
2. "No! That is not the question." Upon receiving this response you simply ask, "Then what is the question?" Let the prospect change the objection into a question that you can answer with benefits.
3. "I don't *have* a question." In this rare event, knowing that every blocking objection *is* a question, you have every right to say, "There may not be a question in your mind, but there *is* one in mine, or you would want to buy! Is the question? . . ." Restate the objection in another way, and ask, "Is that the question?" Probably the prospect will answer with a question like, "No! That is not the question. The question is . . ." Then you will have the prospect's own question to answer!

ANALYZING THE TREATED-QUESTION TECHNIQUE

This Treated Question skill is so rare that at this moment of first exposure it would not be at all unusual for you to be asking some of these questions:

1. Is this procedure unlike going around in unnecessary circles?
2. I still don't understand exactly what we are trying to accomplish.
3. Are *all* blocking objections questions in disguise?
4. How important is it for me to learn to perfect this technique?

Whenever prospects become defensive, they are a micro-second from arguing with you. It is as though prospects mentally draw a line at their feet, and in a boxing stance with fists up say, "Don't step over that line!" Should you challenge prospects, you are very likely to lose!

125

However, should you be able to turn the objection into a question *in the prospect's mind,* all of those defenses can become completely immobilized. Rather than arguing with the prospect, you figuratively get across the line of defense on the prospect's side and reason together!

The prospect gains the upper hand with valid objections if the salesperson does not get the opportunity to present additional benefits. This is why it is so important for a professional to be skilled with a variety of communicative techniques that can relax the prospect and, at the same time, avoid unnecessary conflict.

This instrument is another important conditioning step in handling objections, which keeps you in the role of a professional who thinks in terms of the prospect—first, last, and always! Your objectivity, as well as your empathy, are truly called upon when handling objections.

This technique first of all forces you to face a crucial question! That question is: *"Would the prospect benefit in buying my product despite a blocking objection?"* If so, you should endeavor to win the prospect over to your way of thinking. If not, you should advise him or her not to buy.

The Treated Question openly poses the key to its success, which is: "Would you benefit despite this concern?" If the prospect agrees that this is the question, you have the opportunity to answer it!

EVERY blocking objection is a question in disguise. That question is: *"Would the prospect benefit despite his or her concern?"* No matter how serious any blocking objection may be, the question is would the prospect benefit enough to make the purchase anyway? For you to get maximum effectiveness from this proven technique, this premise must be understood!

Another important consideration of the Treated-Question Technique is that it places the salesperson in the important role of a professional counselor. With the objectivity and empathy this technique demands, prospects are helped to see their opposition to buying from a more practical, unemotional perspective.

Let's dwell for the moment on *overcoming* objections. This misnomer is erroneously used again and again in the selling profession. *Overcome* implies to outwit or fight. It is vitally important to avoid confrontation. Blocking objections are *valid*, at least in the mind of the prospect. You usually cannot eliminate or invalidate them. You certainly cannot overcome them.

Some salespeople think overcoming objections means to immediately change the features or the circumstances to satisfy the prospect's objection. Certainly, limits exist as to how much you are going to be able to reduce your price just because the prospect says it is high. You don't change a prepared program every time you hear an objection. Nor do you redesign a product because of a concern about a feature. Certainly, your company expects you to sell the product, service, or idea *as is!* One of the advantages in using good techniques to handle and answer objections is that it helps the salesperson to sell the features initially presented in the interview.

More Practice on the Treated Question

Because of its unusual nature, this technique takes a bit more concentration and practice until it becomes easy for you. The real benefit will be your ability to salvage sales situations that most salespeople would abandon as hopeless. You will discover many situations where a sale can be made that can repay you for the effort in learning to treat objections as questions.

First, an example using the Treated Question in the generic and alternate forms.

PROSPECT: "We'll stay with our old equipment a bit longer!"

SALESPERSON: "That brings up a question. The question is: Would you *benefit despite this concern*? Is that the question?"

OR

127

"That brings up a question. The question is: '*Would you benefit enough* by investing in new equipment now?' Is that the question?"

Now, let me set the stage for your own practice. Your prospect has held firm on the objection and, in effect, has said, "I'm not going to buy *because* . . ." On the other hand, you feel that if the prospect understood all the benefits of your proposal, this blocking stance would soften or change. You need to have the opportunity to explain those additional benefits. It is time to use the Treated-Question Technique.

PROSPECT: "I can't afford it!"
SALESPERSON: "That brings up a question. The question is . . . Is that the question?"

PROSPECT: "I must have a quicker delivery!"
SALESPERSON: "That brings up a question. The question is . . . Is that the question?"

PROSPECT: "I intend to shop around!"
SALESPERSON: "That brings up a question. The question is . . . Is that the question?"

See! It is not so difficult. Practice this technique with your family or friends the next time you get into an argument. If anything will prove its value to you, being able to quickly resolve conflicts in these situations can do it.

Through experience, once you find how much easier it is to answer objections by considering them as questions *for more information*, you will fall in love with this technique, too!

I'm always concerned when presenting the Treated-Question Technique that it will appear difficult to the salesperson. *It isn't!* In fact, it is one of the easiest to master once you understand what you are trying to accomplish. Might I add, I truly believe it is the most effective skill you can use in handling objections. It does, however, require practice.

We have spent two chapters learning how to handle objections diplomatically before answering them. By now, you should begin to realize that the process of *answering* objections is almost anticlimatic. The next chapter will deal primarily with answering objections, as well as with classifying them.

CHAPTER SUMMARY

Have you gained confidence in dealing with objections? Because this chapter deals with one of the more sophisticated techniques to understand, review what you have read by answering this question:

What was the one most important idea you received from this chapter, and how are you going to apply it today?

Your answer to this question might be:

- Empathy Cushions (*I, He/She, They*) help you to relax the prospect prior to answering the objection.

- "Yes, but" or "Yes, however" is very argumentative. Learn to keep these phrases out of your sales interviews.

- Any real, blocking objection *is* a question in disguise. The question always is: *"Would the prospect benefit enough to buy despite the concern?"*

- If your prospects recognize their objection (which may be blocking them from buying) is actually a *question* in disguise, then you will be given the *opportunity* to answer it.

129

- The Treated-Question Technique is another way to avoid confrontation with the prospect. With it, you do not challenge a belief, and, at the same time, you respectfully give the prospect credit for intelligence.

- The key question to the Treated-Question Technique is: *"Would your prospect benefit despite this concern?"*

- Until you can comfortably rephrase a prospect's concern, use these exact words: "That brings up a question! The question is: *Would you benefit despite this concern*? Is that the question?"

- Expect one of three responses from the prospect with the Treated-Question Technique: "Yes," "No," or, "I don't have a question."

- Remember, it is impossible to overcome a prospect's objection. Overcome means fight! Win an argument with a prospect and lose a sale.

CHAPTER 12

The Reality About Objections

IT IS perfectly normal to fear the unknown. An objection often looms before a salesperson like the Bermuda Triangle. You know it's there, but you don't quite know what to do about it.

The sales field is littered with the debris of lost sales because salespeople avoided or feared objections, or had simple misconceptions of their true nature. The purpose of this chapter is to gain a professional perspective about objections. We will learn that most are predictable, understandable and can even be classified. Once you learn how to classify them, objections are a flight plan right through the Bermuda Triangle. We have already learned that, like the Bermuda Triangle, many objections turn out to be pure myth and certainly nothing to fear.

One major misunderstanding about objections is that too many are considered unanswerable or hopeless. If you approach objections from this perspective, encountering them can be daunting. Hopeless objections are *unanswerable*, and luckily, they are quite rare and seldom experienced in the field. For example, if you call upon a company and are told it can't buy from you because it is entering bankruptcy, the objection is unanswerable and the situation is hopeless. However, you don't really need anyone to tell you this, and little effort needs to be wasted analyzing the meaning of this kind of objection.

Let's release some anxiety by nearly dismissing the hopeless category from serious consideration. Too many salespeople and sales managers, unfortunately, classify quite resolvable objections in this category, thereby conceding an opportunity to sell. In this chapter, we will focus on objections that *are* resolvable . . . and *all* the remaining objections ARE!

The two major types of resolvable objections are (1) those that are *stated* and (2) those that are implied, or *unstated*. Let's look at both.

Of these two general types of objections, it is easy to imagine the unstated is the more treacherous to handle. It is impossible to answer an objection that has not been articulated. Therefore, you must smoke them out by using such techniques as we learned in Chapters 10 and 11—using Obviously You–Jes Supposin' and the Treated Question.

Once these objections are out in the open, (and stated), five distinct categories of objections can be answered:

The groundless objection
The vocal pause
The excuse
The sharp buyer
The sincere objection

The groundless objection. This kind of objection is *not* based on logic or fact. It is extremely touchy because the dogmatism usually used by the prospect suggests emotional involvement or prejudice. Use of the words *always* or *never* in an objection is an almost sure sign of a groundless objection. Or, these words may be implied in the objection. For example:

Your prices are always higher.
Your delivery is always slower.
Japanese products are better made. (Implied)
I'll never get used to the new style.
I don't buy anything over the phone. (Implied)

The four steps to take in answering a groundless objection are:

1. Recognize it for what it is!
2. Cushion your response.
3. Try to show how the prospect's view is inconsistent with something he or she already believes.
4. Drop it and move on.

An example of a groundless objection insurance representatives complain about is, "The Lord will provide!" Since emotions are deeply involved in this objection, it needs to be handled very carefully.

Use steps 2 and 3 to counter.

PROSPECT: "The Lord will provide!"

SALESPERSON: "Mr. Prospect, I admire your faith. Something, though, is troubling me. Tell me, do you carry a spare tire in the car you drive?"

PROSPECT: "Certainly."

SALESPERSON: "The question that bothers me is just where is the line of demarcation of responsibility? I'm not trying to be facetious, nor irreverent, but like your provision of a spare tire in your car, is it possible that insurance protection for your family is your responsibility, too?"

Is this illustration potentially explosive and dangerous? Of course, it is! This particular objection can be hazardous because of strong religious beliefs held by the prospect. Demonstrating the inconsistency in the client's thinking may be the only way to communicate in a rational manner when confronted with the emotional conflict of a groundless objection.

The vocal pause. Sometimes prospects facetiously state objections they don't really mean. Although said in a serious tone of voice, this kind of objection is usually irrelevant and unreal. The prospect's purpose in this meaningless chatter is either to throw

133

the salesperson off track or to slow down the pace of the interview. Also, sometimes a vocal pause can be used by the prospect to hide a blocking objection.

The vocal pause is sometimes referred to as static. The prospect is usually toying with you and may or may not know you are aware of it. This objection will be quickly buried when the Obviously You–Jes Supposin' Technique is used. It will disappear before you cross the dotted line in Figure 2. For example:

FIGURE 2

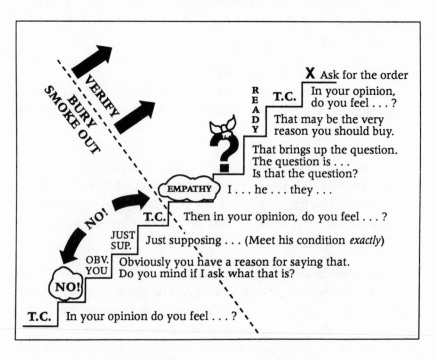

PROSPECT: "I pay so much in taxes now I don't know what I'd do with the extra income."

SALESPERSON: "Obviously, you have some reason for saying that. Do you mind if I ask what it is?"

PROSPECT: "I was just kidding!" (Vocal pause buried.)

Sometimes, the vocal pauses are so flippant, one can just smile and disregard the objection. It can be treated frivolously as long as the prospect knows that YOU know it isn't serious. It is still, though, a category of objections that needs identification.

The excuse. Unlike the *vocal pause*, this kind of objection is said with more conviction. Most of the time, prospects seem very serious when giving you an excuse. If you challenge them, they will defend a statement vigorously, even though it is not their real problem.

Prospects might offer hundreds of excuses that, on the surface, sound very logical and blocking. Our problem is to determine whether such objections are real or not. For example:

I need to talk it over with my partner.

My CPA needs to see this before I buy.

Our new budget comes up two months from now.

Decisions such as this are made only when we are not in our busy season.

You would not be too far wrong to suspect that *most* objections you receive are *excuses*! This excuse objection will rarely get beyond the dotted line in Figure 2. It, too, is usually buried with the use of the Obviously You–Jus Supposin' Technique. Once the excuse is buried, the blocking objection will usually emerge! Sometimes, however, the blocking objection remains obscure until the Treated Question is used.

The sharp buyer. The arrogance and argumentativeness exhibited by the prospect with this kind of objection annoy most salespeople. Conflict often exists because the prospect, after reading a bit about the product, seems to pretend to have more knowledge about the product than the salesperson does!

Don't complain if you are lucky enough to get a *sharp buyer*. Here is an accident waiting to happen! You are hearing buying signals! The only reason the prospect has taken the time to

135

study your product is because of a deep interest in buying . . . from the first salesperson who will listen. With this objection, all that is needed is a little application of the Law of Psychological Reciprocity and the Law of Challenging Belief. For example:

PROSPECT: "The burner in your furnace is mounted too high in the heat exchanger."

SALESPERSON: "Obviously, you have some reason for saying that. Do you mind if I ask what it is?"

PROSPECT: "I read that the neutral point of combustion should be as low as possible for the best economy of operation."

SALESPERSON: "Just supposing that the stack temperature indicates maximum efficiency, as ours does. Then, in your opinion, do you feel you will have maximum efficiency?"

PROSPECT: "I hadn't considered that! How soon could you get your installers to my home?"

SALESPERSON: "Would Monday be soon enough?"

The sincere or blocking objection. Finally, we are down to the category of objections that requires logical answers to eliminate the stumbling block to the decision. Some call this kind of objection *real*; others call it *sincere* or *genuine*. It seems that *blocking* is the most descriptive designation, since it identifies it as the objection real or imagined, which is blocking the prospect from saying, "Yes!"

Properly answering this kind of objection with Units of Conviction to the complete satisfaction of your prospects will usually completely disarm them, and provides a psychological moment to close! It does *not* mean the objection has been eliminated or overcome. Even after an objection is answered, it still exists. But, despite its presence, a prospect might then understand it is in his or her best interest to buy.

Remember, a prospect cannot be emotionally moved to buy

unless first logically convinced such a decision is justified. Answering blocking objections satisfactorily simply convinces your prospect of the merits of the decision to buy.

FOUR TIMES TO ANSWER OBJECTIONS

1. *When* they're raised
2. *Before* they're raised
3. *After* they're raised, . . . and
4. *Never!*

When. *Most* blocking objections are answered *when* the prospect brings them up in the interview. It is normal practice to respond immediately to the prospect's concerns. Objections are a sign of interest. One way for a salesperson to know whether or not he or she is on the right track in the interview is by careful attention to any points of disagreement as they occur.

Before. If you repeatedly receive the same objection from several prospects, you can be pretty certain it is going to happen in future interviews. You disarm the prospect if you handle and answer this recurring objection before it is brought up. This method also gives you credibility early in the interview. The objection has far less weight if the prospect doesn't have to raise it!

After. Two separate, distinct situations in which objections are answered *after* they are raised are:

1. When you don't know the answer.
2. When you had planned to answer it later.

When you truly don't know the answer, say so! Say, "I'm sorry, I really don't know how to respond to that concern. I'll be glad to find out and tell you later."

Your prospects will admire you for your candor. Also, they often take a little pride in being able to stump you, and might become friendlier. Don't fret. No one is expected to have all of the answers. Be certain you do report back with the right answer, though.

Another situation in which you might answer an objection *after* it is raised is when you intend to cover it a little later in the interview. First, ask for permission. Say, "I'm often asked that, and had intended to cover it a bit later. Do you mind if we discuss it in a few minutes?"

Delaying the answer to the objection can sometimes help the planned continuity of your presentation. Most prospects are very thoughtful and do not mind waiting for the answer. Be certain that you *do* return to the objection later, or the prospect will give the concern much more credence than it deserves!

Never. All blocking objections deserve your handling and answering except, perhaps, the vocal pause. This kind of objection can be ignored as long as the prospect is aware that you know he or she is not serious.

Suppose a wealthy individual kiddingly said, "I can't afford it!" Should you know them not to be serious and, more importantly, know they realized you are aware of their frivolity, you might smile and go on with your interview and never answer the objection.

FIVE WAYS TO ANSWER OBJECTIONS

For the preceding two-and-one-half chapters, we have been primarily involved in *handling* objections. Although we discussed the answering of groundless objections, we generalized our references as to what is involved in answering other kinds of objections until we learned to uncover the blocking one. Now, finally, we have arrived at *answering* objections! Are you breathless in some anticipation of a magical way to solve this dilemma? Since the theory of overcoming objections has been exploded into oblivion, are you still looking for some reasonable alternative?

Just as we found the secret to closing was not in knowing *how*, but *when*, we will discover that answering objections, too, is anticlimatic. Success with objections depends not so much on *how* to answer them as it does on finding *which* objection needs answering. There truly is no ONE answer to a specific objection, since the same objection might be answered differently with different prospects. Memorizing an answer for each objection, therefore, does not always work! However, *one* professional attitude does prevail in answering objections. Answering a blocking objection should not be attempted unless your attitude is that, despite the objection, the prospect will profit by buying.

As stated before, a salesperson with even minimal experience has learned the basic rationale of answering objections from other associates or from daily exposure to the objections. Good product knowledge is also an essential foundation for a logical response in answering most objections.

Five methods of answering objections go beyond expertise in product knowledge. They can provide the skills that diminish the impact of the objection upon the prospect while convincing the prospect of the benefits to buy. An easy way to remember these five methods is with the use of mnemonics—READY. We are now READY to answer objections.

These five methods are:

1. *R*everse it.
2. *E*xplain it.
3. *A*dmit it.
4. *D*eny it.
5. Ask, "Wh*Y*?"

Reverse it. Just suppose, for the moment, you could take the force of the blocking objection and turn it back on the prospects as the very reason to buy! You will be absolutely amazed how often the blocking objection can be exactly why prospects should buy. When prospects feel they can't afford something, a potential money-making proposal might be the very reason they should invest! When prospects feel they haven't the time, a potential timesaving product might give them more time! Often, you can let the power of the objection work for you with the technique known as the Reverse Wrench.

That is the very reason you should buy! . . .

Or, in using understatement, "That *may be* the very reason you should buy! . . ." Then, after the Reverse Wrench, the very next word you would naturally use is *because!* This should lead you directly into a Unit of Conviction, followed by one or more Magic Questions. For example:

Whenever my prospects say: "I can't afford sales training," I immediately know they need it more than most!

PROSPECT: "Yes, the question is being able to afford sales training."

SALESPERSON: "That is the very reason you should invest in yourself

because

the average increase in sales and income in 11 short weeks is 38 percent

which means to you

more money in your bank account and quickly.

The real benefit to you

will be your ability to get your new car sooner!"

"In your opinion, do you feel you would like to get that convertible you've been talking about when the new models come out?"

140

When you form the good habit of using the Reverse Wrench, you may find yourself closer to consummated sales than you think is possible!

Explain it. Certainly, the most common method of responding to an objection is to explain your viewpoint of why the prospect should buy. As in the example above, a Unit of Conviction follows the Reverse Wrench and is the professional means of explanation. In each Unit of Conviction, two benefits are offered to convince the prospect of the advantages of buying, despite the concern voiced in his or her objection.

Before an objection is answered through explanation, many Units of Conviction may be required to win the prospect over to your way of thinking (see Chapter 8). You may also need to use one or more of the forms of evidence.

After explanation, the prospect's temperature should be tested with Magic Questions. I repeat, one of the best psychological moments to get the order is immediately after the prospect's blocking objection has been answered to his or her satisfaction!

Let's look at another example of the process of explanation. Assume you have a blocking objection from an associate whom you are trying to sell on joining you in a voluntary civic activity. The objection is lack of free time. You have already confirmed this with Obviously You–Jes Supposin' and both an Empathy Cushion and the Treated Question:

PROSPECT: "Yes, that is the question! I don't have enough time with my family now."

SALESPERSON: "That may be the very reason you should volunteer

because

your family might take great pride in your contribution to the community,

141

which means to you

they can also feel a part of the civic-minded effort.

The real benefit to you

can be the satisfaction one gets only through civic activity."
"Mayor Simms told me the other day that he couldn't think
of anyone who had more organizational experience that is
needed for our task than you! He specifically asked me to see
if you might volunteer."
(Evidence)
"In your opinion, do you feel a little civic activity would be
personally satisfying to you?"
PROSPECT: "There is no doubt I would enjoy it."

SALESPERSON: *"In your opinion, do you feel* your family might
proudly agree to spare some of your time with them for such a
worthwhile project?"
PROSPECT: "How much actual time did you say this project might
take?"
(Buying signal)

In the Explain It phase of answering objections, some or all of
the four questions posed in Chapter 8 may need to be answered
before the prospect is completely convinced.

Those questions were:

1. What is it?
2. How will it benefit me?
3. How much does it cost?
4. Can you prove it?

Admit it. You admit to the validity of an objection when it is
obviously true. If your price is higher than a competitor's, admit it!

If your service is a bit slower, admit it! After you admit it, then you must explain (with Units of Conviction) the benefits of buying. Admitting the truth of an objection is another way of maintaining your credibility. For example:

SALESPERSON: "Yes, this tire is a bit higher in price! It is worth the extra investment

because

it has a 60,000-mile guarantee,

which means to you

more miles of usage for your dollars invested.

The real benefit to you

can be the peace of mind of greater safety when you travel with your family on vacation."

Admitting an objection is not agreeing that it is a cause for not buying. We've repeatedly stated the professional attitude of thinking in terms of the prospect's interest—first, last, and always. If you *agree* with your prospect's objection and cannot offer benefits to answer the objection, then tell them to buy elsewhere. However, when you still believe the prospect should buy, admitting the truth of an objection often opens the prospect's mind to your conviction that there are benefits that justify the purchase.

Deny it. You deny an objection when it impugns your honesty or integrity, or that of your associates or your company. Such rare objections are usually delivered in a harsh, unequivocal way to provoke you. In such a confrontational atmosphere, remember, there probably is something buried deeper in the past causing this outburst. A professional remains diplomatic. Use of Cushions, Obviously You—Jes Supposin', and the Treated Question can soften your reply. Once the cause has been softened, a strong denial *plus* explanation of the truth as you know it may be required.

I've often said, "Salespeople try too hard to be nice!" A stern denial of an untruth about you or your company is sometimes the only way to gain respect.

Ask, "WhY?" The Y in our mnemonics refers to objective questioning rather than the use of "why" that we strongly advised against in Chapter 10. The Y refers to an ability of sometimes letting prospects answer their own objection! Some salespeople are particularly adept at this. Rather than talking when an objection is raised, they ask guiding questions of the prospect until he or she becomes satisfied. For example:

PROSPECT: "Your two-week delivery date on registers will be too late."

SALESPERSON: "When will you have the foundation finished?"

PROSPECT: "In about five days, and the studding will be done in a couple more."

SALESPERSON: "Normally, how long do the finishing and painting take?"

PROSPECT: "The average time is more than a week ... I guess maybe two weeks IS soon enough! Go ahead and place the order."

PUTTING THE STEPS IN HANDLING OBJECTIONS ALL TOGETHER

It can be very helpful to study the potential chronological sequence in handling, analyzing, classifying, and answering objections (developed in all three chapters on objections) by following the step-by-step procedure in Figure 2.

Putting the sequence together, step-by-step, may first appear to be quite extensive and perhaps a little difficult. By practicing it in this manner, you can get a better understanding of the function of each technique and then discover the versatility it offers you!

All of the steps could be used as shown in Figure 2, especially if the prospect is very rigid and opinionated in wanting to defend an objection. However, I would be the first to tell you that I do NOT follow this rigid procedure in most situations! Sometimes when hearing an objection, I might only use Obviously You—Jes Supposin'. Another time, I will sense the need to use: "That brings up a question. The question is . . ." In other circumstances, I might begin: "That is the very reason you should! . . ."

The beauty of completely understanding the purpose of each technique until you can choose the moment of optimum use is that you can have complete choice and maneuverability in the interview! You then learn to apply the techniques either sequentially or individually. My greatest wish is for you to be able to experience this confident feeling of command, but not obvious command, when confronted by objections! It only takes a little study and practice.

Now, with an eye on Figure 2, follow the entire stair-step sequence starting with the Trial Close:

SALESPERSON: *"In your opinion, do you feel* the new national TV advertising campaign will make the product a profitable one for you to promote?"
(Trial Close)
PROSPECT: "I most assuredly wouldn't risk stocking another product at this time!"
("Explosive NO!")
SALESPERSON: "Obviously, you have some reason for saying that. Do you mind if I ask what it is?"
(Obviously You)

PROSPECT: "The board of directors has recommended major cut-backs in inventory due to the current market conditions."

SALESPERSON: "Just supposing, for the moment, this was not a concern, then *in your opinion, do you feel* the new national TV campaign might make this product a profitable one to promote?"

(Jes Supposin')

PROSPECT: "Usually, I wouldn't hesitate on introducing such an item with such extensive backing, but I don't want to go against the board's recommendation until market conditions change."

SALESPERSON: "I understand your caution. Other companies have indicated a more careful monitoring of their inventory. That brings up a question. The question is whether or not you can promote this profitable item and stay within your board's recommendations. Is that the question?"

(*I-They* Cushion plus Treated Question)

PROSPECT: "It certainly is the question!"

(Reverse Wrench plus Unit of Conviction)

SALESPERSON: "That is the very reason you should join our promotion

because

we deliver within only a couple of days from the moment we receive your order. We also can do your stocking for you,

which means to you

that your salespeople can start selling this item tomorrow.

The real benefit to you is

you will be able to report profits to the board at your meeting next month."

PROSPECT: "What did you say the standard markup on this is?"

SALESPERSON: "Fifty percent! *In your opinion, do you feel* this makes it very attractive?"

(Trial Close 2)

PROSPECT: "The board of directors will appreciate good news such as this!"

SALESPERSON: "Would a gross of each color be a minimal amount for you?"

(Order-Asking Question)

Now, following the example above, fill in the blanks with your own complete step-by-step handling and answering of an objection:

SALESPERSON (Trial Close): "*In your opinion, do you feel . . .*"

PROSPECT: "No!"

SALESPERSON (Obviously You): "Obviously you . . ."

PROSPECT: "Your price is unreasonable!"

SALESPERSON (Jes Supposin'): "Just suppose . . . then (Trial Close), *in your opinion, do you feel . . .*"

PROSPECT: "I still don't intend to pay that much."

SALESPERSON (Cushions): "I . . ."

SALESPERSON (Treated Question): "*That brings up a question. The question is . . . Is that the question?*"

PROSPECT: "That is the question."

SALESPERSON (Reverse Wrench plus Unit of Conviction): "That is the very reason . . ."

SALESPERSON (Trial Close): "*In your opinion, do you feel . . .*"

PROSPECT: "Are monthly payments available?"

SALESPERSON (Answer plus Order-Asking Question): . . .

Practice the stair-step approach to handling objections with an associate until it becomes easy for you to respond effortlessly and automatically. Review the purposes of each technique until you understand when and how they apply. Notice how each technique complies with the Law of Psychological Reciprocity and the Law of Challenging Belief.

In summary, this chapter has dealt with the handling, analyzing, classifying, and answering of objections. Let's review an outline of the material so you can check your own comprehension.

Two major kinds of objections one might encounter in a selling day are:

1. The hopeless objection that *cannot* be answered.
2. Those objections that *can* be answered.

Of those objections that *can* be answered, two types are:

1. Those that are *not stated*, and must be smoked out.
2. Those that *are stated*.

Of those objections that *can* be answered and *are* stated, five categories are:

1. The *groundless objection*
2. The *unfounded vocal pause*
3. The *excuse*
4. The *sharp buyer*
5. The *sincere* or *blocking objection*

Four times to answer objections are:
1. *Before* they're raised . . .
2. *When* they're raised . . .
3. *After* they're raised . . .
4. *Never!*

Five ways to answer an objection are:
1. *Reverse* it.
2. *Explain* it.

3. *Admit* it.
4. *Deny* it.
5. Ask, "WhY?"

This chapter completes our discussions of the Conviction Step begun in Chapter 8. We have exhaustively concentrated on the logic of the presentation in which we convince prospects of the merits of our product, service or idea, and its benefits.

If, along the way in our interview, the prospect still hasn't bought, with the successful completion of the Conviction Step, the prospect should be mentally thinking, "It is a good product and it would benefit me. It is priced right, and if I really *want* it, I will be justified in buying!" Sometimes, however, the order is not forthcoming until we create the desire to cause them to WANT it. How to create desire will be explored in Chapter 13.

CHAPTER SUMMARY

Please stop for a moment, reflect upon the past three chapters on objections, and then answer this question to enhance your own feeling of accomplishment. I expect, perhaps, a different response from each reader!

What is the one most important idea you have learned in handling, analyzing, classifying, and answering objections?

Some important points in this chapter were:

- Hopeless objections are unanswerable, but fortunately they are rarely encountered in the field. They cannot be answered.
- Objections that can be answered fall into two general categories: (1) those that are not stated and, (2) those that are stated.

- Those unstated must be smoked out (with Obviously You–Jes Supposin' or the Treated-Question techniques).
- Can you name the five different categories of stated objections?
- Can you name the four times to answer objections?
- Can you name the five ways to answer objections?
- The most common way to answer an objection is to explain it. You now can excel at this by using Units of Conviction!
- Think of each step on the stair-step analogy as a distinct, separate arrow in your selling quiver to be used *separately* as you see fit. The stair-step shows the potential maneuverability of all the techniques in sequence.

CHAPTER 13

Creating Desire

CUSTOMERS BUY from emotion, not by logic! To this point, much of our examination of the sales process has supported this statement. Any experienced salesperson will also acknowledge its truth. That brings up a question. The question is: "How much emotional appeal do you incorporate in your sales presentations to help your prospects decide to buy?" Is that the question?

I have asked this question in all of my classes. Most students admit they give very little or no consideration to including emotional appeal during an interview. Even the most experienced, who should know the value of creating desire, make similar confessions. Taking the time and effort to learn how to incorporate the power of motivating prospects through their emotions in your sales repertoire can, in fact, place you in a category above the more experienced!

If we acknowledge that customers buy from emotion, not logic, a more accurate question to ask ourselves at this time is: "How do salespeople *ever make* a sale if they disregard the motivating force that causes their prospect to buy?" A quick answer is: "*If* the sale was made, the prospects have taken the Desire Step on their own." This answer does not account for missed sales that *could have been made* had the salesperson known how to include the step during the interview.

This chapter deals with the all-important Desire Step in the sales process. We introduced the importance of emotional appeal in sales situations in Chapter 5 when we learned about dominant buying motives. Remember it was said, "If you know a

151

prospect's dominant buying motive, the sale is 70 percent over." We also learned that if all of the bridges in the Unit of Conviction (Chapter 8) are used conscientiously, the buyer's benefit *usually* appeals to the emotions of the prospect. If you have been practicing these two emotional building blocks, you have probably experienced some positive results from appealing to your client's emotions.

The strategies of creating emotional appeal in the Desire Step will take us much further in our ability to sway a prospect's opinion in our favor. Emotional appeal takes place when one or more of the five senses are involved. Emotionally to move prospects, you must help them to see, hear, feel, taste, or smell the happy end results of enjoying your product, service, or idea.

Recall Cruikshank's two reasons that prospects do *not* buy:

1. They are *unaware* of their problem.
2. They are not *sufficiently disturbed* by it.

The Desire Step addresses these two barriers to a sale by a three-part process. First, it reminds prospects of their problem, or opportunity, and gets their agreement that it *is* a problem. Second, it reminds prospects that your proposal will solve their problem. And, third, through emotional appeal, it invites them into wanting to take immediate action because you paint a vivid word picture in which they imagine themselves using, enjoying, and benefiting from your proposal. For example:

"You are determined to be the #1 producer in your company. Is that correct?"

"Concentrating on the sales principles in this book will enable you to achieve this goal quicker than you might suspect."

"It's six months from now. You have effectively been in

control, but not obvious control, of a sales interview that could result in the largest sale of your career. You become aware of sudden friendliness from your prospect, and notice she is touching her chin. You hear her say to an associate, 'This is really what we have been searching for, isn't it?' She reaches across the desk and you feel the firm handshake of congratulation. You know for certain the sale is yours, and inwardly you feel excited that this order puts you over the top in your company's sales contest!"

"This is what you really want, isn't it?"

THE DESIRE STEP

This step consists of three distinct parts:

1. First, *remind* your prospect of his or her problem, and get agreement.
2. Second, *remind* your prospect that your proposal will solve the problem.
3. Third, *paint* a word picture of an end result. Utilize at least three senses in which the client can imagine using, enjoying, and benefiting from your proposal. Then, ask a question to ascertain whether or not the prospect envisions the picture.

The Desire Step seems to be an entirely new concept to most salespeople. Therefore, it is not redundant of me to repeat its functions until they are understood and appreciated: (1) It reminds prospects of their problems (or, paraphrasing it—*opportunities*); (2) gets their agreement; and (3) then helps them vividly to fantasize their enjoyment of buying through the use of concrete language, appealing to their senses, which disturbs them enough to want to take action NOW!

Concrete Language

In the third part of the Desire Step, *concrete language* is used. This term applies to language that appeals to any or all of the five senses—sight, hearing, tactile touch, smell, or taste. Concrete language helps you to produce visual images in the prospect's mind through the painting of descriptive word pictures that appeal to the senses.

Concrete language is the opposite of the specific, logical language prominently used to be convincing in the Conviction Step: "You will appreciate the flexibility of this plan" is specific, logical language. "You *feel* relaxed and comfortable as your financial goals are achieved and *see* your equity gradually increase in our monthly reports" is concrete language.

In many situations, prospects need the inspiration of a professional salesperson enabling them to envision the satisfactory end results of buying. The Desire Step, or fourth step of the sale, is a sophisticated one, which requires your perceptive, intimate understanding of each prospect. With this understanding and your execution of the intricacies of this step, you will be head and shoulders above your competitors who rely on logic in their sales presentations!

Read the use of concrete language I just received in the mail from a magazine, attempting to inspire me to join their sales promotion contest:

> Mr. DuBois, returning your sweepstakes gives you a chance to win $5 million. Imagine what that could mean to the DuBois family. No more worries about bills. You could live how and where you wished. And you'd have plenty left to buy all the luxuries you've ever dreamed of. Believe it or not, all this could come true if you mail your sweepstakes acceptance certificates today!

If this kind of language works for them in motivating people to take action, why wouldn't it work equally well for you?

Sound difficult? It isn't at all. Let me put you in a picture of a vacation in Hawaii. See if you experience some of the emotions brought about by my word pictures. Can you:

See? The sandy beaches of Waikiki, the blue sky, and people surfing on the white foaming waves.

Hear? People laughing and playing along the shore.

Feel? The warm, gentle breezes coming off the ocean.

Taste? The tartness of a Mai Tai drink combined with a shrimp cocktail.

Smell? The salty ocean breezes, mixed with the aroma of broiled mahi mahi cooking on a nearby grill.

Depending upon both my ability to use descriptive language, and whether this scene appeals to you, this concrete language might cause you to take action.

Now, let's practice your own natural abilities in the use of concrete language. I'm going to ask you to describe a happy moment in the past—a time and place to which you would most like to return. Use your imagination and write in descriptive language, using any of the five senses, which might apply to your mental picture of that pleasant occasion. What do you . . .

See . . .

Hear . . .

Smell . . .

Feel . . .

Taste . .

In fact, you regularly utilize concrete language in normal conversation when telling friends and associates of interesting events! Therefore, since you have this ability to make the *past come alive*, in creating desire you simply use this ability through the use of concrete language to make the *future come alive!*

Bridges in the Desire Step

If there is still indecision in the interview after a prospect has been convinced in the Conviction Step, it is because the mental picture of a satisfactory end result is not strong enough to move the prospect emotionally to an immediate decision. Therefore, it is imperative that all word pictures be in the *present tense* so that the prospect feels the urgency of the moment to make a favorable decision. The major purpose of the Desire Step is to cause your prospect to *see* the desirable results of buying now!

The bridges in the Desire Step are designed primarily to keep you in the PRESENT TENSE so that the prospect envisions the benefits of taking action *now*. Notice the placement of the bridges in the three-part process:

1. *Mrs. . . . you want . . . Is that correct?*
2. *This . . . will do it.* (Insert your own product, service, or idea.)
3. *You own this, and this is what happens. It's* (time). *You are* (place). (Now paint word pictures appealing to at least three senses.) *This is what you really want, isn't it?*

Putting It Altogether

Carefully read the next example of the three-part Desire Step, noting the step-by-step progression and the use of the italicized bridges:

"Mr. Brown, somewhat earlier you stated that *you want* dependable and efficient heating comfort in your home. *Is that correct?*"

"*This* two-stage gas furnace *will give you* exactly that!"

"*It's* the middle of February. *You are* looking out your living-room window at the worst snowstorm of the season. Even when standing next to the glass, your feel the warmth of the room provided by the perimeter system. You walk to the thermostat and hear only its quiet click as you nudge it up a degree or two. You remember commenting to your wife about the lower heating bills you've been receiving. You say to yourself, 'This is great!' "

"*This is what you really want, isn't it?*"

Now, for your own exercise in imagination. Think about a prospect you have been trying to motivate toward an affirmative decision in your favor. Determine as best as you can the primary interest, or problem AND the dominant buying motive, or emotional impulse. Let your imagination run free. Picture what this prospect might see, hear, taste, feel . . . a mental picture of enjoyment! Then, fill in the blanks to creating desire:

As I understand it, you want . . . Is that correct?
This . . . will do it.
You own this/buy this/agree with this, etc. and this is what happens!
It is . . . (set exact time, date) and you are (set location). You (paint word picture-present tense).
This is what you really want, isn't it?

The Timing of the Desire Step

Sometimes the use of the Desire Step is crucial to the success of an interview. An analogy might help to better understand how often emotional appeal is needed in your sales presentations. This fourth step of the selling process is somewhat like the *X* on a typewriter keyboard. The *X* is not used too often in main copy, but a skilled typist knows precisely how and when to use it when it's required. Like the typist, the professional salesperson must be ready and able to use the Desire Step when it becomes necessary! *It is required only when prospects are unable to envision the advantages of the end use of the product on their own.*

Let's identify more specifically *when* the Desire Step is necessary. Interestingly, the prospect sometimes unwittingly signals the exact time to appeal to the emotions! You might hear something to this effect: "Well, I know this is probably the right thing for me to do. But, I just *don't want* to get involved right now!"

Read between the lines to what was just said. It sounds like the prospect is convinced (Conviction Step logic is accomplished). However, the prospect seems to be having trouble envisioning strongly enough the satisfaction of buying to substantiate making an immediate decision. The operative words you should hear in such a response from a prospect are *"don't want."* It is your responsibility to use the Desire Step in such a situation to cause the client to *want* to buy now!

Especially in those presentations when an inordinate amount of time was spent in the Conviction Step, it is possible to overburden the prospect with logic. The prospect can become confused and feel the need to procrastinate in order to sort out the facts and details before buying. The timely use of the Desire Step at this moment can be crucial to inspire immediate action to buy. Frequently, the consummation of the order is but a paragraph or two away!

In short, anytime you sense the prospect has lost the dream (motivation, vision, or promise) of enjoying the use and benefits of buying the emotional inspiration reproducing this dream in his or her mind might be necessary (the Desire Step).

Years ago, Marie Brachman, a salesperson for Aid Association for Lutherans Insurance Company, excitedly reported back after a session on creating desire. She said she had spent a good deal of time trying to convince a couple to use her plan for retirement only to meet with inertia and apparent uncertainty. She decided she would try an emotional appeal.

"Mr. Smith," she said, "as I understand it, both of you are planning to enjoy your summer home in Upper Wisconsin when you retire. Is that correct?"

"We would like to if we can afford to retire," he replied.

"This retirement plan we've been talking about all evening might make this possible!" she asserted. "You own this plan, and this is what happens," she continued. "It is ten years from now. You awaken from a restful night sleep here in your home. The warm sun is brilliantly streaming in through the windows. At first, you're startled, until you realize you no longer have to go to work. You're retired! You smell the delicious breakfast Martha is preparing, and as you leisurely walk into the kitchen you say, 'Martha! Let's pack quickly, hook up to our new fishing boat and trailer, and go up to Door County for some fishing!' "

Marie said she noticed a smile on his face, and a faraway look when he abruptly said, "Where do I sign?" The Desire Step had caused the hesitations to disappear!

Remember, the Desire Step is not a "selling" step . . . it is an emotional appeal. It is not product oriented . . . it is people oriented. It does not get into the nuts-and-bolts features of the product . . . it appeals to the dominant buying motive by describing through the senses the pleasant and satisfying end results of a favorable decision to buy!

The emotional impulse that causes the prospect to take action must occur before the decision is made whether you create it through emotional appeal or the prospect senses it on his or her own. A truly professional, sophisticated salesperson has the knowledge and the ability to cause it to happen whenever it is necessary!

CHAPTER SUMMARY

To appeal successfully to the emotions, a salesperson must have a thorough understanding of the process and a keen imagination. Answering the following question and reviewing the important features of this chapter might help perfect both!

What was the one most important idea you received from this chapter, and how are you going to apply it today?

Some of the more important features were:

- Customers buy from emotion, not by logic!
- Anyone can make the past come alive with concrete, or descriptive, language. In creating desire, this innate ability is focused on making the future come alive for the prospect.
- Concrete language is language appealing to the five senses— seeing, hearing, feeling (tactile), smelling, and tasting.
- Remember, the Desire Step consists of a simple three-step process. Describe it in your own words.
- All word pictures must be in the *present* tense because you want the prospect's emotions to cause them to buy NOW.
- The Desire Step bridges should not be altered because they are designed to keep you on the selling track, and to speak in the present tense.
- The Desire Step should automatically be used *if* the salesperson senses the prospect is unable to *visualize* the end result of buying (dominant buying motive).

CHAPTER 14

Handling the Procrastinator

HAVE YOU ever had prospects who seemed unable to make a decision no matter how hard you tried to convince them? Did you leave the interview confused about their hesitancy, wondering whether or not there was something else you could have done to salvage the sale?

Although there is nothing unnatural about procrastination, salespeople often become frustrated when some prospects can't seem to make up their minds. Usually the salesperson gives up far too easily, often at the very moment the prospect could be helped and a sale made!

We shouldn't be impatient or resentful when faced by a procrastinator because the prospect can be experiencing emotional conflict and possibly even trauma about the pending decision. Rather, the salesperson's response to procrastination should be one of genuine empathy. Remember, *empathy* means being able to put yourself in the other person's shoes without becoming emotionally involved. The resulting objectivity can help you recognize the prospect's emotional state of mind and adapt an appropriate sales presentation.

How do we help to resolve the mental conflict of indecision? A salesperson must dispassionately draw back from the situation and attempt to relieve the apprehension a prospect feels when faced with a difficult decision. We do this by introducing the weighing process called the Procrastinator Close at the end of the sales presentation. It provides an excellent *summary* that objectively compares the pros and cons previously discussed during the sales interview.

The technique developed in this chapter can be used to lighten the mental anxiety of prospects who cannot seem to make a decision. It brings the emotional conflict and the trauma of indecision out into the open where they are easier for the prospect to face. The real benefit to you is that it enables you to summarize and close a lengthy sales presentation!

The Procrastinator Close is a time-tested technique. Even Ben Franklin used a form of this technique in a Socratic method of decision making. The process has been called by several names—Ben Franklin Close, Weighing Close, Summary Close. However, labeling it the Procrastinating Close seems best to identify when it should be used, and tends to suggest what it accomplishes.

In a lengthy presentation, it is not unusual for a prospect to become confused and indecisive when trying to assimilate all the information. Comments such as, "I'll have to think about it," "I never make up my mind the first day," or "I probably should shop around a bit" are red flags of indecision. Any such vacillation can be your lead-in to using the Procrastination Close.

Recognizing a procrastinator's inner conflict in the summary of your interview enhances your credibility in your prospect's eyes. Objectively summarizing the negatives along with the positives gives you an incredible advantage in closing. Notice how this is done in the following example:

PROSPECT: "It is a big decision. Perhaps I should sleep on it!"
SALESPERSON: "I surely understand your concern! Before any intelligent person can make a decision, the *ideas opposed* must be weighed against the *reasons for buying NOW!* Let's do it in this case."

"On the *ideas opposed* side, you were concerned about the price of the investment . . . whether this is the right time for you . . . and you also mentioned some other priorities for your business!"

"Let's compare these with the *reasons for buying NOW!* On the reasons for buying side, you realized this to be a very profitable item for you . . . you liked the convenience of our service . . . and you were impressed with the limited amount of inventory you would have to maintain. You especially were pleased with the fact that our product could quickly become a sales leader for you, which would also help to attract new customers for your other products."

"Which, in your opinion, do you feel outweighs the other, the *ideas opposed*, or the *reasons for buying NOW?*"

PROSPECT: "It surely might cause more customer traffic. How soon could it be delivered?"

Let's examine some new and unfamiliar terms used in the example.

Ideas opposed. These are objections that *have already been handled and answered* to the prospect's satisfaction during the interview. After an objection has been properly handled and answered, it is technically no longer an objection but an idea opposed. Referring to these negatives as *objections* tends to give them too much credence and weight, and certainly this word should not be spoken in the closing process. The phrase *ideas opposed* infers that the objections have been somewhat diminished in importance since they were previously handled and answered earlier.

Never fear bringing up negatives near the end of a long interview! If your prospect hasn't bought after your Conviction Step or Desire Step, these negatives are apparently still present and contributing to the procrastination. If they are allowed to remain submerged, they tend to grow in importance with time. Bringing them out into the open in the closing summary diminishes their force on the prospect since you don't allow them to become "bottled up."

Reasons for buying NOW! In the weighing summary, these reasons are a listing of all, or perhaps most, of the benefits that were enumerated during the Conviction Step of the sales presentation. We learned in Chapter 8 benefits tend to be "heavier" than logical facts because they are often emotional in nature. In this weighing process, *reasons for buying NOW!* are also heavier than *ideas opposed*. Ideas opposed are negative facts that are "lighter," too, since they are logical. This phenomenon helps to strengthen the salesperson's case by balancing emotion with logic in the Procrastinator Close.

Some salespeople like to change the phrase *reasons for buying NOW!* to *reasons for investing NOW!"* since almost all buying decisions are investments of some form or another. Either phrase is very effective.

If it is possible, the *last reason for buying NOW!"* should be centered upon the dominant buying motive. This places the strongest motivating force at the end of the sales presentation, and many times can tip the scale in favor of the salesperson.

Salespeople utilizing the Procrastinator Close often draw a vertical line down the center of a tablet in the presence of the prospect. They list *Ideas Opposed* on the left, and *Reasons for Buying (Investing) NOW!* on the right. Then, they develop the weighing process by directly involving the prospect in the analysis. Study the following Procrastinator Close, and imagine it being cooperatively developed with the prospect.

SALESPERSON: "Joan, before making a decision, let's weigh the *ideas opposed* and compare them with the *reasons for investing NOW!* We'll list them on this tablet."

Ideas Opposed	Reasons for Investing NOW!
Cost	A new, fresh approach
Time involved	More enjoyment at work
Change in habit	Less frustrations
Others?	Easier access to information
	Better end product
	Most of all, personal pride in accomplishments
	Others?

"Now, Joan, as we look at the two lists, which, in your opinion, do you feel outweighs the other—the *ideas opposed*, or the *reasons for investing NOW?*"

Analyzing examples of the Procrastinator Close should disclose several subtle features:

- The lead-in bridge alerts the prospect to the procedure of comparing pros and cons.
- The prospect's concerns (*ideas opposed*) are listed with candor and sincerity. (These concerns should be listed with no emphasis . . . almost in a monotone!)
- The prospect may be asked for "Others?" to be certain *all* concerns are out in the open.
- The *reasons for* . . . are listed last. (It is hoped with some enthusiasm!)
- The last *reason for* . . . centers on the dominant buying motive.
- If you ask for "Others?" in *ideas opposed*, to be fair the prospect should be asked for "Others?" in *reasons for* . . ." (If your prospect gives you *one*, you have a *strong buying signal!*)
- Immediately following the comparison of the two columns, you have an excellent opportunity to probe with a Trial Close!

165

WARNING! Do *not* attempt to "answer" the *ideas opposed* when listing the *reasons for buying NOW! This is not a selling (convincing) process* . . . it *is* a summary. Look again at the example, and you'll see there was no rebuttal whatsoever with responses to the negatives. To avoid this common mistake when first using this technique, it might help if you cover up the left column while enumerating the benefits on the right.

One of the greatest advantages of this technique is that it helps you to understand when you have done about all you can do for the prospect. If the prospect *still* says, "I'll have to think about it!" you should graciously yield to his or her preference of not making an immediate buying decision. After all, it is the client's decision to make, and you need to know when to "fish or cut bait." Sometimes salespeople need help in recognizing when further efforts of selling are futile! With this weighing process, however, the odds are greatly stacked in your favor.

Referring to the examples again, let us intently review how the Procrastinator Close can bring order to the confusion facing the prospect by empathetically summarizing the decision-making process. The advantages of this procedure are:

1. At first, they might assume they will be left alone to "think about it," only to discover that together with the salesperson, they will think about it *out loud, and NOW*.
2. They hear the salesperson's understanding of their mental dilemma.
3. Prospects may be impressed by the honesty of the salesperson in reviewing their blocking ideas opposed with candor and objectivity!
4. With their negative factors out in the open, prospects lose much of the apprehension of a buying decision.
5. Prospects hear the principal benefits reviewed in comparison with the ideas opposed.

Let's compare your advantage in using this weighing procedure against what *might* have taken place had you truly given up and allowed prospects to "think about it." Whenever you allow prospects "off the hook" to think *only* about these negatives, you are almost guaranteed an ultimate failure of a lost sale. After all, because they know the *ideas opposed* very well, that is what they think about! Because of your expertise with your product's features and benefits, you understand the *reasons for . . .* better than your prospects. It is, therefore, to their advantage to be reminded of them.

Your first practice of the Procrastinator Close could be done by recalling a prospect who was unable to make up his or her mind about buying. Use a lined tablet to create an abbreviated list in the left-hand column of all the objections you handled during your interview with this individual. This should be easy to do since the prospect gives you these comments for free! One usually needs to concentrate a bit more when listing the benefits in the right-hand column.

If you use your own tablet, draw a vertical line down the center of the page. Then list all the features and benefits under *Reasons for Buying NOW!* at the top right. Remember, the last benefit should be centered around your prospect's dominant buying motive, if you know it!.

Conclude with your Trial Close: "Which, *in your opinion, do you feel* outweighs the other—the *ideas opposed* or the *reasons for buying NOW?*"

Before practicing the technique aloud or with an associate, take the time to select a comfortable bridge to your weighing close. You may wish to develop your own or use one of the following:

"Before making a decision, one must weigh the *ideas opposed* side with the *reasons for buying NOW* side. On the *ideas opposed* side . . . Now, on the *reasons for buying NOW* side . . ."

167

"I understand your concern! Before any intelligent individual can make a decision, the *ideas opposed* must be weighed against the *reasons for buying NOW*! Let's do it in this case. On the *ideas opposed* side . . . Let's compare this with the *reasons for buying NOW* side . . ."

"I can surely understand your wanting to think about it. Let's think about it out loud now! On the *ideas opposed* side . . . Let's compare this with the *reasons for investing NOW* side . . ."

The purpose of the bridge in the Procrastinator Close is to identify exactly what you are doing so that the prospect can quickly follow the procedure. This is especially important if you use the weighing process *verbally* without the use of paper and pencil.One of the most memorable reports about the use of the Procrastinator Close came from stockbroker Jim McIntyre.

Jim had been frustrated by the number of clients who had rejected his phone recommendations by saying, "Jim, I believe I'll watch it for a while!"

Jim said to me, "Lee, if you allow the prospects to 'watch' an issue, you lose in one of three ways:

1. "If the stock goes up, they feel they missed an opportunity, and should have bought.
2. "If the stock goes down, they are glad they didn't buy.
3. "If the stock remains static, they feel their recommendation didn't have much merit."

Because this dilemma helped neither the prospect nor Jim, he got in the habit of summarizing each phone call with, "Before making a decision, let's weigh the *ideas opposed* side against the *reasons for investing* NOW side . . . on the *ideas opposed* side . . . on the *reasons for investing NOW* side . . ."

Then, after reciting both columns of the Procrastinator Close, he would ask, "Which, *in your opinion, do you feel* outweighs the other? *The ideas opposed* or the *reasons for investing TODAY?"*

Jim reported an immediate increase in orders, and found that his regular clients appreciated the procedure so much they expected him to summarize his recommendations in this manner.

You, too, may be pleasantly surprised just how quick and easy it is to use this technique after you have practiced it a few times. More importantly, you will be amazed how many more sales can be salvaged when you add this technique to your professional selling skills. Your prospects will be pleased, too, because you help to relieve their anxiety of making a big decision!

CHAPTER SUMMARY

Think about the many ways you could use this Procrastinator Close, either at the end of a lengthy sales presentation or as a separate summarizing technique during an interview. Again, the reviewing question:

What was the one most important idea you received from this chapter, and how are you going to apply it today?

Perhaps your answer is one of the following advantages of the Procrastinator Close:

- You should empathize, not become frustrated, by a procrastinator.
- *Ideas opposed* are objections that have been handled in the interview.
- The Procrastinator Close is a *summary* and not a *selling* technique.

- After a lengthy sales presentation, you help the prospect reduce the enormity of a big decision.
- You objectively weigh the pros and cons for the prospect, thereby sustaining an image of fairness.
- In closing, you remain in command, but not obvious command, of the interview.
- You know when your presentation is at an end, and when you have done all you can do!

CHAPTER 15

Putting It All Together

GETTING MAXIMUM results from this book requires more than merely practicing the individual techniques presented in each chapter. Rereading the book will enhance your ability to tie the techniques together in each of your sales presentations. Throughout, we have urged you to practice skills one at a time until they become habitual. Unless you reread the book, it is possible for you to become overwhelmed with the number of techniques presented. Each review will cause the techniques to appear simpler and more practical.

Many graduates of my weekly professional sales training return to repeat the entire program two and three times. At first, I was puzzled by their very common comment, "Lee, I got ten times more out of the course the second time than I did the first!" Gradually, I began to realize exactly what was causing this enthusiastic response. I learned that one's perspective changes each time the course is repeated.

It is important for you to know what to expect the first, second, and third times through this book.

First reading. The technique spotlighted in each chapter appears as a separate entity. The interrelationship between the various skills in other chapters is not immediately apparent. Expect to appreciate most the chapter that provides the answer to your greatest sales problem.

Second reading. Expect to discover the need for a well-planned sales presentation from beginning to end. The interrelationship of techniques becomes exciting and valuable in your

171

preparation for sales interviews. Before each sales call, you should find yourself analyzing the effectiveness of each step of the selling process that you intend to present.

Third or more readings. Real professionalism in presentations develops as you find more maneuverability in the use of the techniques. As selling becomes more habitual, you find the time to listen conscientiously to your prospect's opinions during the interview. Rather than following a somewhat mechanical, step-by-step progression, you pick and choose techniques that fit the situation. By doing this, you maintain command, but not obvious command, of the interview in a sensitive, conversational manner. You become aware of the individual purpose of the techniques and instinctively use them where needed. Even though you preplan each presentation, you are able to vary from your plan whenever it helps you to communicate more effectively. You develop the versatility of using techniques as needed and not necessarily in a sequential manner. Then, and ONLY then, are you truly a skilled professional salesperson!

To assist you in the development of your own sales presentation, what follows is a complete sales presentation containing the five steps: Conversation, Curiosity, Conviction, Desire, and Close. *It is not intended to be a model sales talk,* but this rather abbreviated example is for your inspection and analyzation of the total selling process. The bridges are italicized for your convenience.

"Congratulations on your perseverance in faithfully reading, studying, and practicing the professional sales communication techniques chapter by chapter. It certainly shows your commitment to improve your own abilities so that you can increase your sales performance. It also testifies to your open-mindedness to tried and proven principles."

"... the reason I mention this, we have an ...

... idea that can further improve your effectiveness and cause you to sell easier, more profitably, and more automatically! It will also enhance your professional image and help you to serve your prospects better."

"The idea? ... write out a complete sales talk!"

"Writing a sales presentation is good practice

because

it helps you to formulate continuity of presentation,

which means to you

that you begin to develop better habits

and the real benefit to you is

a more organized and succinct delivery in actual sales talks in the future."

"In your opinion, do you feel a succinct and organized approach will be more successful in future interviews?"

"In your opinion, do you feel better habits are important?"

"In your opinion, do you feel the need for more smoothness and continuity in your sales presentations?

"The more you review each selling principle in the book, the easier selling becomes

because

173

practicing the principles over and over helps you to sell effortlessly and naturally,

which means to you

that your interviews will become more prospect oriented."

"The real benefit to you is

increased sales and income."

"In your opinion, do you feel increased income might help solve a lot of personal problems?"

"In your opinion, do you feel that personalizing each presentation to your prospect's needs is important?"

"In your opinion, do you feel practicing good techniques until they become habitual will make your selling easier?"

Practicing the sales presentation surely paid off for Toney Chimienti as a marketing director for Colonial Life and Accident. Toney said:

"I called on the comptroller of Brock's Department Store, which employs 500 people. The man had a miniature traffic light on his desk! He turned on green for me to start my presentation. When he objected to something during a part of my sales talk, he turned on yellow! After completion of the full step-by-step DuBois techniques in presenting my products, the comptroller turned the light completely off rather than turning on the red, or stop, light! He stood up and congratulated me for being the first salesperson in 14 years not to get a red light. I was given a large order at that moment and was very glad I had prepared my presentation carefully before making that call."

174

Had you made the call instead of Toney on such a tough prospect, do you feel you would have gotten the red light?

For example:

You want to be #1 in your sales organization. *Is that correct?*
Writing out a complete sales presentation and practicing it until it becomes natural to you is the first step!

You do this, and this is what happens. It's a year from now. You are at the company sales convention in the Bahamas. The big sales trophy is being presented, and you hear your name called! Your spouse gives you a quick, excited hug, and you stride to the podium. The president, with a smile on his face, gives you a firm handshake and hands you the shining, gold trophy with your name engraved on it! You hear the applause and see the affection in the happy smiles of your friends and peers. For a moment, you hold the trophy high and you say to yourself, "This makes all of my practicing worthwhile." *This is what you REALLY want, isn't it?*

Before anyone can make a firm commitment to the effort of writing a few sales presentations and practicing them, one has to weigh the *ideas opposed* against the *reasons for investing the time NOW!*

Ideas Opposed	Reasons for Investing NOW!
Takes some time	Practice makes perfect
Takes some effort	Selling becomes more fun
And, some concentration	You sell habitually
Did I leave anything out?	Your prospects profit, too
	You'll make more money
	You'll become #1 in sales!
	Were there any I should add?

175

"Which, *in your opinion, do you feel* outweighs the other, the *ideas opposed* or the *reasons for investing right NOW?*"

"Good! First, you must select the product or idea you intend to present to your next prospect."

Please review this sample presentation:

- Identify the Conversation Step of the sale. Which of the ten ways of getting into comfortable conversation were used? (See Chapter 6)
- Identify the bridges:

  —from the Conversation Step to the Curiosity Step. (See Chapter 7)
  —from the Curiosity Step to the Conviction Step. (See Chapter 7)
  —in the Unit of Conviction. (See Chapter 8)
  —in the Desire Step. (See Chapter 13)
  —in the Weighing Close. (See Chapter 14)

What was the dominant buying motive in this example? (See Chapters 5 and 13)

How many Magic Questions were used? (See Chapters 3 and 9)

Which of the seven forms of evidence were used? (See Chapter 8)

Which of the six types of Order-Asking Questions were used? (See Chapter 3)

Incidentally, did the presentation inspire you to write and practice your own presentation?

Consider the report from Buzz Brescoll, vice president of First of Michigan Corporation in Detroit. Buzz wrote, "After taking your course . . . I slowly changed from a confused, unskilled and unsuccessful nonsalesman, who really dreaded doing 'his thing' every day, to a reasonably competent, confident, successful salesman and sales manager, who loves the selling experience and challenge!"

My reason for quoting Buzz is I personally know the price he paid to excel! Buzz spent not weeks or months, but years reviewing sales techniques. He played audio tapes of our techniques before nearly every call to remind him to use the selling principles.

How can you get maximum mileage from your investment of time with this book? I want to report, and *emphasize*, that the task is easy! Continue to write and practice complete sales presentations until you are satisfied it is no longer necessary. During each selling week, create some reminder for yourself of only one technique or selling principle. It is surprising how quickly each will become habitual. Within a little time, you will be thinking in terms of complete presentations as you prepare for each call.

For example, look over and review the entire stair step in handling objections. Choose Obviously You–Jes Supposin' one week; Cushions the next; the Treated Question next; and the five ways to answer objections after that. In just *four* weeks, you will be proficient in handling objections and looking forward to them in your interviews.

Throughout the book, great care has been taken to present selling techniques in a somewhat rigid, sequential manner! However, I would be the very first to tell you not to follow this format always in every presentation. It is important to know there is a progressive step-by-step, analytical overview of the selling process, but once you truly understand the *purpose* of each technique, and have practiced each until you can use it *habitually*, you should have the freedom to use techniques separately OR sequentially as you see fit.

CHAPTER SUMMARY

Throughout the book, I've tried to "clue you in" to situations that can trigger instinctive responses with the use of good sales techniques. Very often the prospect "tells" you exactly what to do in the interview, but salespeople are often unable to sense these cues unless they can take their minds off themselves and listen more conscientiously. Practicing techniques until they become habitual and instinctive allows one to become a better listener. This sensitivity and maneuverability throughout the interview will be greatly admired and envied by your associates, but *it takes practice!*

Joseph Bubba, an investment broker, having completed professional sales training, summarizes his attitude toward his chosen occupation of selling by saying, "I used to think of selling as an art, but now I consider it a science. A salesperson doesn't have to be born—he or she can be made. Selling is no longer a numbers game of making a lot of calls, but an analytical and selective use of professional techniques!"

Again, the important question of self-examination and analysis! I expect, perhaps, a different answer from each reader.

What is the one most important idea you received from this chapter?

CHAPTER 16

"Secret" to Success!

"SINCE YOU say you have personally trained thousands of salespeople, Mr. DuBois, you surely have found the answer!"

"The answer to what?" I asked cautiously. It was a very tense moment in the middle of an important interview on Wall Street with Mr. Beane, a senior partner of Reynolds & Co. Previously, I had received approval on a sale for my 11-session sales training from the director of training and several other partners. A substantial five-figure check awaited me on Mr. Beane's desk if he gave final approval for a company class.

"Surely, by now, with all your experience," he explained, "you have discovered a common denominator . . . some singular attribute of a top producer?"

Slowly, shaking my head I replied, "Mr. Beane, I really don't know of any."

Mr. Beane smiled, leaned back in his chair, and puffed on his pipe. He remarked that he, too, had been unable to find such a singular, distinguishing trait of a successful salesperson. However, he felt that he had found a common characteristic of average or failure-oriented individuals. He believed, without exception, they were *oversensitive* to their failures. When missing sales, they tended to brood, lose heart quickly, and quit trying, whereas a top producer would say, "Lose one—get two!" . . . and go right back out without hesitation and make more sales calls.

Even though I was fortunate enough to make the sale without all the correct answers, Mr. Beane's question challenged me to begin an intensive search of my own for a distinguishing characteristic of top producers.

Two years later, I made a special return trip to New York to tell Mr. Beane what I had discovered. After a few minutes of reminiscing with him about our class in which he, too, was a student, I said, "The first day we met you really stumped me with your question about a singular trait of a top salesperson. Since that time, I've tried to be more observant, and, I believe, I just may have found your answer! It is simply this . . . show me a salesperson who has a *goal* and I will show you a success! I have found that top sales producers are goal oriented."

The purpose of this chapter is to identify, describe, and define the true meaning of goals, and then reveal a five-step formula that you can follow to maintain top production and achieve your dreams!

The secret to success—goals. So easy to say, but so very difficult to get people truly to accept. When I was first exposed to this phenomenon in instructor training, I asked my instructor-trainer why he waited until the last session of our course to introduce it to the class. He quickly replied that less than 15 percent of any class was ready to accept this concept even after we as instructors had earned the right to become almost unquestioned in other matters. His words haunted me all the rest of my teaching career because I have confirmed that he was absolutely correct!

Tell me, are you in the 15 percent category? Is your mind really open to accepting this secret to success? Or, are you already negating the suggestion by assuming that I may be exaggerating or perhaps talking about "pie in the sky"? If so, I challenge you to what could be the most important revelation of your life!

You have undoubtedly heard this appeal to set goals many times, and it has been expressed in countless ways. Salespeople have been preached to, cajoled, and arm twisted on this subject, ad nauseam! Scores of motivational meetings for salespeople have this message as a central theme. Because of redundancy, it seems the admonition to set personal goals virtually "goes in one ear and out the other." Yet, when the process is properly understood, accepted, and followed, it promises one the attainment of the greatest of dreams.

To understand properly the importance of this issue, we are again confronted with the need for a definition. *Goal* is another word somewhat carelessly bandied about in our selling profession with no specific meaning attached. Because it lacks a precise interpretation, this important word can become what I call a *vague specific* and carry little impact.

A goal is the emotional manifestation of the results of your dreams and aspirations.

Perhaps the only synonym that can best describe this word *goal* is *"obsession."* This synonym is the only one I have been able to find that best conveys the intensity and the drive of a goal-oriented salesperson. If you were to observe carefully goal-oriented individuals, as I have, you would find them *obsessed* about their dream as if nothing, but nothing, could interfere with its accomplishment.

Some confusion about goals lies in the common misunderstanding of the difference between *goals* and *objectives*. Goals are NOT logical in their development nor in their nature. Goals are emotional . . . objectives are logical! Goals go far beyond the numbers game that is so often employed for achieving logical objectives.

Therefore, in this specific sense of the word, it might come as a surprise to realize that companies *cannot* set goals . . . they set objectives. Goals, by this extraordinary characterization, are uniquely emotional and personal . . . and therefore, *not* logical. People rarely set goals . . . too often they set only objectives. One cannot achieve the results from goals without first understanding exactly what it means to set them. Could the misinterpretation of the difference between these two words be a reason why so very few salespeople respond to the many exhortations to set goals?

Throughout this book we have emphasized the power of the dominant buying motive, or DBM. We referred to it as the #1 emotional impulse that causes your prospects to buy. Now, we are turning this emotional, impulsive force back on you, since a goal is the *primary emotional impulse that drives you to the success you desire.*

In Chapter 5, we separated needs and wants as being *logical* factors considered in a decision. The dominant buying motive was described as the emotional force that *causes* the decision. Here, we are making a similar distinction between objectives and goals. Objectives may be *what* you logically want or need to accomplish, and are an important consideration in your plans for success. But the goal, or dream, is the fantasized end result of *why* you would want to accomplish it! Setting of goals goes far beyond the setting of quotas or volumes reported in call sheets while attempting to achieve logical objectives. One cannot set a goal without *envisioning* and *sensing* the emotional feelings associated with the successful accomplishment of it!

To enable one to develop a continuous sense of accomplishment and to help keep the striving for success alive and more constant, it is important to divide goals into three distinct categories and stipulate their duration: These three goals should be set simultaneously:

Long-range goal—no longer than five years!
(For example, becoming worry free because of financial independence, moving into a beautiful new home, driving to work in your choice of car.)
Intermediate goal—yearly or biannually.
(For example, receiving a top sales trophy at the company's annual sales meeting.)

Short-range goal—daily or weekly.
(For example, helping two prospects a day with a well-planned
   sales interview.)

Your *long-range* goal should be set FIRST. This goal should be
carefully and painstakingly chosen, then decisively written down.
Be certain to include the *exact* date it is to come true. Once any goal
is reached, then another should replace it. The reason the long-
range goal should rarely exceed five years is that the mind cannot
effectively deal with it as an obsession much longer than that. This
goal should be given the #1 priority it deserves!

The *intermediate* goal should be an incremental stepping-stone
to the five-year goal. It, too, should be dated, then carefully and
decisively written down. Usually, an intermediate goal is set for a
period of one to two years.

The *short-range* goal is the daily or weekly obsession that you
feel is necessary to enable you to achieve the ultimate results of
your long-range goal. This goal provides you means whereby you
can have the important satisfaction of acknowledging daily ac-
complishments toward your long-range goal.

It is usually necessary to decide on the objective before setting
the goal. For example, your *objective* might be to own a Mercedes,
but it is the *dream* of what you sense in your mind's eye while
driving it that is the happy end result that motivates you toward
the accomplishment of your personal goal!

Once your goals have been set, it is important for you to check
your progress from time to time. A periodic review enables you to
revise and fine-tune your short-range and intermediate goals so
that your long-range goal can be more easily reached.

REMEMBER! Never create any goal without writing down, and
memorizing, the exact date that you intend for it to become true. It is
vitally important that your mind becomes obsessed with the goal
and the time frame in which it is to be accomplished. Spend some
quiet time visualizing the pleasing and satisfying results of the goal.

Now, since we have explored the true meaning of goals, and have determined over what time interval they are to be set, the moment has arrived to reveal the "secret" success formula! It is called a secret since so very few people seem to know about it. The formula for success is so powerful that I have little reservation in using a word I seldom use ... I *guarantee* it will work unless sickness or death interferes. Is that strong enough language to get you to consider using it?

Study the formula carefully and pay particular attention to how the steps interlock. Memorize the procedure, and review the five steps from time to time.

THE DPTNL FORMULA FOR SUCCESS

Five steps are involved in this success formula. Do yourself a great favor by taking these steps very seriously. They are:

Decide
Pretend
Treasure map
Never take no!
Listen to your subconscious

Decide! Your mind cannot deliver results unless you very carefully identify your objective (*what* you want), and then develop your goal (*why* you want it). Your goal must envision those parts of the mental picture you would most enjoy having come true. A written goal might sound something like this:

In October 1997, my wife and I will take a trip to Europe. We'll fly to London and enjoy a guided tour of the British Isles. We will then fly to Holland and start a relaxed five-day cruise up the Rhine to Basel, Switzerland. There, we will rent a car and drive leisurely through Switzerland, the Black Forest in lower Germany, and visit many cities enroute to Frankfurt. After a carefree month of travel and relaxation, we will return home. I'll need to save $20,000 for this goal so that all our accommodations can be first class!

Never act impulsively in setting your goals. Take time in thought and preparation. You will be acting upon your decision for a long time, and you want to be certain you will achieve worthwhile results.

Be absolutely certain your long-range goal has #1 priority and that it is extremely important to you. Be very careful you consider all the ramifications of possible fulfillment. Achieving your goals could change your life dramatically! You want to be certain that such change is desirable. If these changes might affect your spouse and family, urge them to help you in deciding on your goals by talking about them.

Pretend! Once you have determined and recorded your goals, relax and *dream* about them. Picture yourself enjoying their fulfillments. Insofar as the senses might apply, think of what you would see (in your mind's eye), hear (in your mind's ear), feel, taste, or smell in the happy picture of end result.

Have you ever gone shopping for a new car thinking you would just check out a few prices? The salesperson insisted on a demonstration ride. You smelled the new interior, noticed the quietness of the car, felt the surge of power from the engine, and admired the beauty of the design. Suddenly, you get serious about the purchase, and practically take food away from the table to own it! Emotions begin to take over from reason.

In several chapters in this book you learned the power of using emotional appeal on your prospect. Now, I am turning the power of emotions on you! Once emotional images of your success are strong enough to become an obsession, then you have set a goal.

What kind of pictures do you have on the screen of your mind about your future? Do you wake up each morning thinking: ". . .

back to the grindstone!" Or, do you picture yourself making an important sale and helping a prospect and yourself?

"The pictures you hang on the screen of your mind are what you are . . . no more . . . no less," I've implored thousands of my students. "And, it is the picture you feel most strongly about that will come true first!"

"What you see is what you get!" a famous TV actor used to say again and again. In a much different context, and in regard to goals, my comment to that statement is: "Precisely!" How do you *see* yourself a week from now, a month, a year, or five years? Have you even thought about it? Goals, once they become an obsession, can be translated into what you see, hear, feel, taste, and smell in a mental picture of end result of enjoying the fruits of your labor! They can be expressed in an exciting, vivid word picture of your dreams of whatever represents "success" to you.

During your most creative time of the day, establish the habit of envisioning your enjoyment in the achievement of your goals. You must *repetitiously* set in motion this emotional appeal to the subconscious, which is responsible for motivating you to the achievement of your dreams.Whenever possible, act as though your goal is happening NOW! Stretch your mind by pretending how you will react once the goal is realized. Will you view your career opportunities differently? Will you strive even more to perfect your daily work habits? Will you upgrade your require-ments when classifying the kind of prospect you will call upon in the future? Will you spend more time with your family? What *will* you be doing differently to help you achieve this goal, and just how will success affect YOU?

Treasure map it! Surround yourself with reminders of your goals. In the example of the goal of the European trip, one might get travel folders of places to visit. You should surround yourself with pictures of the goal, perhaps keeping them in front of you on the dashboard of the car or framed on your desk. Seeing them often can work on the subconscious. Do everything you can to keep a visual reminder of your goals close to you until your dreams become an *obsession!*

Never take "no!" Should self-doubt sneak into your mind, eradicate it immediately! If you feel your goal is becoming unattainable, mentally give yourself a scolding. Never allow negative feedback from your subconscious to remain in existence over any measurable period of time. Use either audible or inaudible affirmation to give battle to such negative thoughts.

Do not confide your goals to anyone who might tend to discourage you. Only tell them to those who are inclined to say, "I know you can do it!" Sometimes our closest, most well-intentioned friends or family discourage us without knowing it. Have you ever heard someone say, "Take it easy! You'll live longer." That innocent bit of advice is a solid "no!" to any important goal.

This is not to suggest you should be a workaholic. Actually, your short-range goals give you a consistency of effort that makes the attainment of long-range goals relatively easy. However, if your predetermined objectives and goals are discouraged by others, NEVER TAKE "NO!" FROM ANYBODY.

Listen to your subconscious! Now, for the strongest admonition of all in causing this process to work for you! Learn how to hear that quiet voice of inspiration within you. Listen to your subconscious. It usually speaks to you at your most creative time of day.

When does the subconscious speak to *you*? You can usually identify the time by pausing to reflect upon when you prefer to do your daily planning of activities. Some of us plan our activities and organize our thoughts early in the morning, perhaps in the shower or over a cup of coffee. Others organize their work in the evening before going to bed. Still others need to keep a pad and pen by their bed to capture creative thoughts in the middle of the night that might otherwise be lost!

My wife and children have long known never to bother me with major decisions after 5:00 P.M.! "Ask him in the morning," my

187

wife would counsel our children. On the other hand, I know better than to bother my wife with important matters during the early morning hours. "So," I've joked, "we only talk about serious matters at noon!"

The reason it is important to know your most creative time of day is because this is when your *subconscious* usually speaks to you! This is when it provides the creative answer that will some unsuspecting day tell you *how* to proceed to reach your goals. You really don't have to know exactly how you'll accomplish your goals when you initially set them. Your subconscious will tell you once your obsession has taken over.

Stop right now and identify your most creative and productive time of day. This is very important! It is amazing how very few salespeople have given this any thought at all. Your awareness of this time of heightened sensitivity will enhance your ability to tune in to inspirations from the subconscious. Learn to listen to it!

I remember one real-life situation when the emotions of a daily goal salvaged the successful career of a failure-oriented salesperson burdened by the company's pressure of logical objectives.

I once visited my friend George West, who was a division manager with Prudential Insurance. He was worried about having to fire a young salesperson, Ed Lange, who was five days away from losing validation because of insufficient sales.

When I asked George what activity was required of a newly hired representative, he quickly said, "Salespeople like Ed are supposed to set a *goal* of *40 cold calls* a week, which will result in *ten interviews!*"

Can you imagine the enormity of these *objectives* in the minds of new salespeople? Would you like to have to worry about making 40 cold calls every week during your lifetime career? Wouldn't you be exhausted before you started, regardless of the proven logic of this objective? How many insurance salespeople do you suppose have crumbled under the pressure of this seemingly impossible task?

That afternoon I had the opportunity to talk with Ed. I have never seen a more disconsolate, discouraged, or disillusioned person.

"Ed, who helps whom with an interview? Do prospects help you by letting you present your insurance ideas, or do you help them by getting them to think about their financial future?" I asked.

"It works both ways," Ed replied somewhat sarcastically.

"Exactly!" I said. "Ed, I suggest you concentrate on *helping* your prospects and try to take your mind completely off your own troubles. I want you to *forget* about 40 cold calls a week or about your need for ten interviews. All I want you to do is *help two people a day* with a complete interview . . . whether they buy from you or not! If you do this, I'm certain you can become a member of the Million-Dollar Roundtable in two years' time, and be able to afford the things you want to buy for your family."

"O.K., I'll do it," he said. He started for the door!

"Wait a minute, Ed," I cautioned. "Now, this must become an obsession with you. Realize if you complete the two interviews you are a hero; but if you get only one, you are a bum!"

He quickly nodded and again started for the door.

"Wait a minute, Ed," I repeated. "If you only get one interview today, don't try to make up for it tomorrow. Just back up to the kicking machine and make certain you help two people with complete interviews the next day, all right?"

"Right!" he said, and bolted from the room.

The next morning George excitedly told me Ed had made two sales the previous evening! "I only asked him to get two interviews," I astonishingly replied. "I know . . . and he sold them both." George laughed.

Within four months, Ed was fourth highest in sales in an agency of 60 salespeople. In two years' time, he had qualified for the Million-Dollar Roundtable. Shortly thereafter, he was selling $2 million of insurance per year.

Later, I had the opportunity to visit Ed in his private office and congratulate him. "Ed, are you still helping two people a day?" I asked. "Naw!" he replied. "I now help four a day!"

Ed may have not understood the word *goal*, but he became self-motivated by a short-range daily obsession that translated into long-range results. He must have quickly envisioned the importance of helping others, and thereby helping himself. He must have pictured himself receiving the membership to the Million-Dollar Roundtable and hearing the applause and accolades from his manager and associates. I'm absolutely certain he no longer worried about the *objective* of 40 cold calls a week.

Could the obsession of daily goals be the main answer to *organization* that management keeps talking about? How many people do you need to *help* each day to achieve your long-range goal? You realize, don't you, that anytime we are not in front of a prospect, we are virtually unemployed in our chosen profession of selling?

The "secret" to success—*goals!* Goals are an obsession! The pictures you hang on the screen of your mind are exactly what you are, no more, no less! Goals—the emotional manifestation of dreams and aspirations! I beg you to take this chapter seriously and develop your success pattern by setting goals.

CHAPTER SUMMARY

What is the one most important idea you learned from this entire book? I definitely expect a different reply from each person.

It is my hope this book has helped to advance the cause of professionalism in selling for all who read it. Perhaps this emphasis can restore a bit more pride to some who become discouraged from the pressure of the selling day.

It is hoped some of these ideas and techniques might enhance the professional image of all salespeople. This book should help all to hold their head up high, proud of what they do in helping their fellowman, and themselves!

It has often been said that nothing happens in our free-market world until a sale is made! The wheels of our economy are virtually geared to the American salesperson. In that sense, therefore, our nation's prosperity is directly placed upon your shoulders and mine.

You should know, as a professional salesperson . . .

Your future is unlimited . . .
The world is your territory . . .
Mankind is your business . . .
And, God is your boss!

APPENDIX A

Guide to "Let the Customer Buy"

Lee DuBois has developed a professional sales technique video course titled "Let the Customer Buy." This exciting course corresponds very closely to this book. Each of the 16 sessions is approximately 30 minutes in duration.

This guide will enable you to compare chapter titles in the book with the corresponding tape in the videocassette course.

Everyone Sells! (*Chapter number and title*)	**Let the Customer Buy** (*Videocassette number and title*)
Chapter 1 "Myths and Modern-Day Realities"	I. Introduction "The Science of Consultative Selling"
Chapter 2 "It's the Law!"	II. Professionalism "Customers—First, Last, and Always"
Chapter 3 "The 'Secret' of Closing the Sale"	VII. The True Secret of Closing "Knowing When to Close" IX. Let the Customer Buy "Order-Asking Questions"

Chapter 13   XIII. Creating Desire
"Creating Desire"   "The Strength of Emotional
                                       Appeal

Chapter 14   XIV. Weighing Close
"Handling the Procrastinator"   "Eliminate: 'I Want to Think It
                                       Over'"

Chapter 16   XVI. Goals
"Secret to Success!"   "The 'Secret' to Your Success!"

For more information on the video course, please contact:

Manufacturing, Distribution,   Gray Media, Inc.
and Software companies   P. O. Box 424
                                   Exeter, New Hampshire 03833
                                   800-497-3060
                                   603-778-9212
                                   FAX 603-772-7817

All other companies   Lee DuBois Technologies, Inc.
                                   110 Boggs Lane, Suite 100
                                   Cincinnati, Ohio 45246
                                   800-658-0055
                                   513-771-2788